Competition in The Oil Industry

$4.95

This book addresses the following questions: Are oil and other energy industries highly concentrated? Have independent distributors of gasoline lost their market shares in recent years? Do vertical and horizontal integration pose serious threats to the competitive viability of the industry? Similarly, what has been the effect of joint ventures, exchange and processing agreements, and interlocking directorates on competition in the oil industry?

What monopolistic power is exercised by the integrated oil companies because of their control of pipelines and the relatively high entry costs in refining? Finally, have the oil industry's profits been excessive? Do these profits indicate anti-competitive behavior on the part of the industry?

The research for this book was sponsored, in part, by a grant from the National Science Foundation, Office of Energy Research and Development Policy. Work on this study began in the Fall of 1974 and was completed in January of 1976.

OCCASIONAL PAPERS ON ENERGY POLICY
Volume I

Competition in The Oil Industry

William A. Johnson
Richard E. Messick
Samuel Van Vactor
Frank R. Wyant

ENERGY POLICY RESEARCH PROJECT
The George Washington University, Washington, D.C.

For information address:

Energy Policy Research Project
The George Washington University
2031 "F" St., NW
Washington, D.C. 20006

This paper was written, in part, under a grant by the National
Science Foundation, Office of Energy R & D Policy. The authors are
(or have been) associated with The George Washington University's
Energy Policy Research Project. The comments contained in this
paper reflect the view of the authors and not the National Science
Foundation.

International Standard Book Number   0-916862-01-1

Library of Congress Catalog Card No.   76-8263

Contents

Summary

Is the oil industry competitive? On its face, this question seems rather straightforward. Either the industry is workably competitive or it is not. Yet, the question of competition in the oil industry has provoked debate almost since the formation of the first oil company in 1861. Critics of the industry have pointed to one set of indicators as proof of monopoly; defenders have pointed to another as proof of competition. Policymakers have been caught in the middle, bombarded by studies and bewildered by the conflicting claims of experts. As a result, the issue has never been resolved. Nor has the debate ended.

Now, because of high prices, shortages following the Arab embargo, and complaints by some oil companies, competition in the oil industry has again emerged as a major issue of public policy. Hearings are being held by several committees of both Houses of Congress. Legislation has been introduced that would break up the largest companies. The Federal Trade Commission staff is now prosecuting the eight largest U.S. oil companies for antitrust violations, and several academicians have written treatises arguing for drastic restructuring of the oil industry.

This book addresses the following questions: Are oil and other energy industries highly concentrated? Have independent distributors of gasoline lost their market shares in recent years? Do vertical and horizontal integration pose serious threats to the competitive viability of the industry? Similarly, what has been the effect of joint ventures, exchange and processing agreements, and interlocking directorates on competition in the oil industry? What monopolistic power is exercised by the integrated oil companies because of their control of pipelines and the relatively high entry costs in refining? Finally, have the oil industry's profits been excessive? Do these profits indicate anticompetitive behavior on the part of the industry?

Among the more important conclusions of the book are:

- The oil and other energy industries are among the least concentrated in the United States. Based on this measure alone, there would appear to be little reason for special antitrust legislation aimed at the industry.

- The assertion that major oil companies are encroaching on the independent marketers' share of gasoline sales is not supported by the facts. Some independent marketers have lost ground. However, as a class, it would appear that independent marketers have actually increased their share of gasoline sales in recent years.

- Arguments that vertical integration lessens competition in the oil industry are without foundation. In fact, vertical integration is one reason why the various segments of the oil industry are relatively unconcentrated. It also enables lower costs to consumers and helps to assure the relatively smooth functioning of the various operations required to convert crude oil in the ground into gasoline at the pump.

- The argument that the involvement of oil companies in other energy activities is anticompetitive is equally without foundation. In fact, horizontal integration provides maximum flexibility in investment in alternative sources of energy. It also permits oil company expertise to be used in other energy industries.

- Joint ventures between otherwise competing oil companies are relatively common in the exploration and production of crude oil. The few studies that exist of the competitive effects of these ventures do not suggest a pattern of anticompetitive behavior. In fact, these ventures serve an important role in helping to spread the high risks associated with exploration for crude oil. In the absence of joint ventures, drilling activity would decline and the public would have to pay more for the oil it consumes.

- There is little evidence that major oil company ownership of pipelines promotes anticompetitive abuses. Pipelines are regulated as common carriers and any complaints about unfair treatment can be taken to the Interstate Commerce Commission. There have been few complaints in recent years.

- Exchange and processing agreements are available to independent as well as integrated oil firms. Again, there is little evidence that these agreements have been used to dampen competition in the oil industry. In fact, they benefit the consumer by minimizing transportation costs and enabling efficient use of existing refining capacity.

• Directorate interlocks in the oil industry do not pose a serious anticompetitive threat. The argument that it does credits boards of directors with far more influence than they generally have. Moreover, it presumes that collusion by other means is impossible if, indeed, oil companies were inclined to violate existing antitrust law. In general, the study finds that objections to interlocking directorates are unconvincing.

• Entry barriers have not been insurmountable. Where they have been most significant, in the refining sector, they have often been the result of government policies—not industry behavior or structure.

• Finally, the oil industry's rate of return, particularly when measured over a relatively long period of time, has differed little from the average rate of return for all U.S. industry. There is little evidence that the industry's profits have been excessive or "obscene," as some industry critics have charged. There is also little evidence of monopoly profits having been earned by the major oil companies.

Perhaps the most important overall finding of the study is that many of the alleged anticompetitive practices in the industry are not the result of collusion, but can be traced to often ill advised policies of local, state, and national governments, as well as various regulatory bodies in Washington. The book stresses throughout that the real issue facing the nation is greater U.S. energy self-sufficiency. Attempts to punish the oil industry for alleged anticompetitive behavior are contrary to the national interest, if for no other reason than that they detract from the achievement of this goal.

Introduction

Because of sharply higher prices, shortages of oil following the Arab embargo, and complaints by some independents that they are being put out of business, there has been growing dissatisfaction with the oil industry, particularly with the major oil companies. Although public concern over recent developments is understandable, these developments are primarily the result of actions by the Organization of Petroleum Exporting Countries (OPEC) and especially the Arab countries. But, as is often the case in times of adversity, it is easier to attack the enemies within rather than the more distant and less assailable adversaries abroad. And, to many in the United States, the most visible enemies within are the major oil companies.

For this reason, during the past two years there have been a number of proposals to stiffen regulation of the oil and gas industry. At the federal level, much of 1974 was spent in debating the Consumer Energy Act, a bill that, in some of its incarnations, would have reduced the oil and gas companies to the status of public utilities.[1] The 94th Congress is considering a number of bills that would establish a federal energy production company and require divorcement of certain industry activities. Several states have introduced legislation or sponsored referenda that would also increase regulation of the oil and gas industry. The purpose of this book is to discuss the various arguments given for greater regulation of the industry and whether these arguments are correct.

---

1. *Hearings on the Consumer Energy Act of 1974 before the Senate Commerce Committee,* 93d Cong., 2d Sess., pt. 4, 1974, p. 1357. Also *Oil and Gas Journal.* April 15, 1974, p. 19.

CHAPTER ONE

Concentration in The Oil Industry

Is the oil industry monopolistic? Assessing the level of monopoly power in an industry is a difficult task. The primary problem is that there are many views about what monopoly is and how it should be measured; no single measure is universally accepted. There is the additional problem that what is a monopoly in one situation may not be in another. And, while it is difficult to measure monopoly in one industry, it is even more difficult to make cross-industry comparisons.

Yet, to many critics of the oil industry as well as many men on the street, the energy industries are obviously controlled by a few large companies. For example, Congressman (and announced presidential candidate) Morris Udall has asserted: "By any reasonable criteria of what constitutes a concentrated industry. . . the energy industry qualifies and is in clear violation of the intent of the antitrust laws."[1]

Congressman Udall is correct in one sense. Because monopoly generally involves one or a few sellers in control of a market, it has become customary to measure monopoly in terms of concentration ratios. By definition, a concentration ratio is the percentage of assets, value added, or output accounted for by a specified number of the largest companies in an industry. Government studies of monopoly have traditionally used concentration ratios based upon value added by the largest four or eight companies in an industry.

---

1. *Oil and Gas Journal.* April 28, 1975, p. 31.

In the interest of consistency, the government definition of concentration is adopted here. Where value-added data are not available, we use alternative measures to compute concentration ratios. However, the underlying principle remains the same, whether the concentration ratio measures the percentage of reserves of a resource held or the dollar sales of a product. For a specified number of companies, the higher the concentration ratio, the greater the monopoly power in an industry. The greater, also, will be the justification for imposing special controls on the industry.

Concentration ratios are by no means a foolproof measure of monopoly power in an industry. A few large, dynamic companies may provide more effective competition in an industry than many small, static companies. The chain supermarket vs. the corner grocer is an example often cited. Even so, concentration ratios remain one of the most widely used measures. Where monopoly power is found, it often involves a small number of companies in control of an industry. Also, the smaller the number of dominant companies in an industry, the easier for these companies to follow a price leader and arrive at tacit agreements concerning output.

Table 1 contains the percentage of reserves, production, refining, sales, shipments or capacity accounted for by the largest companies in various energy industries. Tables 2 and 3 present concentration ratios for other industries. These data indicate that the oil industry is no more concentrated than other energy industries. Perhaps more significant, all energy industries, including oil, are far less concentrated than many non-energy industries. While in 1972 concentration ratios in the oil industry ranged from 29 to 38 percent for the four largest oil companies, in other major industrial sectors these ratios ranged from 31 to 93 percent. While the four largest oil companies controlled 31 percent of U.S. refinery output, the four largest companies controlled 87 percent of the output of chewing gum, 74 percent of the output of chocolate and cocoa products, 70 percent of the output of greeting cards, and 90 percent of the output of electric lamps. Based on concentration alone there would seem to be greater reason to regulate as monopolies the chewing gum, chocolate, greeting card, and electric lamp industries. And, if these examples seem trivial, the largest four companies producing primary copper, flat glass, and motor vehicles accounted for 72, 92, and 93 percent of their industrial output respectively in 1972. These industries are just as basic to the economy but are far more concentrated than the oil industry.

Nor does it appear that the various segments of the oil industry have become more concentrated over time. (See Table 1.) The one exception is the increasing share of large companies in crude production between 1955 and 1972, a trend that reflects, in part, the

2

TABLE 1
CONCENTRATION RATIOS FOR MAJOR SECTORS OF THE ENERGY INDUSTRY OF THE UNITED STATES

Sector	Percentage Accounted for by the Largest 4 Companies	Percentage Accounted for by the Largest 8 Companies
Crude Oil Reserves		
1970	37.2	63.9
Crude Oil Production		
1955	18.8	31.1
1970	30.5	50.1
1972	29.4*	46.9*
Total Crude Oil and Natural Gas Liquids Production		
1972	28.8*	45.8*
Petroleum Refining		
1955	32.8**	57.5**
1972	31.0**	56.0**
Gasoline Sales		
1954	31.2	54.0
1972	29.0	51.6
Natural Gas Sales (interstate)		
1955	23.0	35.0
1971	25.3	42.8
Lubricating Oils and Greases		
1967	38.0**	50.0**
1972	31.0**	44.0**
Uranium Mining and Milling Capacity		
1971	54.4***	78.5***
Coal Production		
1955	16.5	24.0
1972	30.4	40.4

Data from Duchesneau, Thomas D. *Competition in the Energy Industry.* Cambridge: Ballinger, 1975.

Moody's Industrial Manual, Petroleum Engineer and U.S. Bureau of Mines.

**1967 and 1972 Census of Manufacturers: Concentration Ratios in Manufacturing.* Washington, D.C.: Department of Commerce, Bureau of the Census.

***AEC, *The Nuclear Industry,* Washington, D.C.: Government Printing Office, 1971, p. 20.

TABLE 2

CONCENTRATION RATIOS FOR MAJOR INDUSTRIAL SECTORS OF THE UNITED STATES

Sector	Percentage of Value of Shipments Accounted for by the Largest 4 Companies		Percentage of Value of Shipments Accounted for by the Largest 8 Companies	
	1967	1972	1967	1972
Primary Aluminum	.d	79	100	92
Flat Glass	94	92	98	d
Motor Vehicles	92	93	98	99
Primary Copper	77	72	98	100
Tires and Inner Tubes	70	73	88	90
Aircraft	69	66	89	86
Industrial Gases	67	65	84	81
Alkalines and Chlorine	63	72	88	91
Synthetic Rubber	61	62	82	81
Blast Furnaces and Steel Mills	48	44	66	65
Industrial Trucks and Tractors	48	50	62	66
Semiconductors	47	57	65	70
Weaving Mills (synthetic)	46	39	54	54
Ship Building and Repairing	42	47	59	63
Construction Machinery	41	43	53	54
Lubricating Oils and Greases	38	31	50	44
Fertilizers	35	35	55	53
Petroleum Refining	33	31	57	56
Weaving Mills (cotton)	30	31	48	48

d. The government withholds these data to avoid disclosing information about individual companies.

Source: *1967 and 1972 Census of Manufacturers: Concentration Ratios in Manufacturing,* Washington, D.C. Department of Commerce, Bureau of the Census.

4

TABLE 3

CONCENTRATION RATIOS FOR OTHER SELECTED INDUSTRIAL SECTORS OF THE UNITED STATES

Sector	Percentage of Value of Shipments Accounted for by the Largest 4 Companies		Percentage of Value of Shipments Accounted for by the Largest 8 Companies	
	1967	1972	1967	1972
Electric Tubes (Receiving)	94	95	99	99
Electric Lamps	91	90	95	94
Hard Surface Floor Coverings	89	90	99	98
Turbines and Turbine Generators	76	90	82	96
Chewing Gum	86	87	96	98
Primary Batteries	85	92	95	97
Cathode Ray Picture Tubes	84	83	98	97
Cigarettes	81	84	100	100
Typewriters	81	d	99	d
Sewing Machines	81	84	92	92
Gypsum Products	80	80	93	93
Chocolate and Cocoa Products	77	74	89	88
Household Vacuum Cleaners	76	75	94	91
Woven Carpets and Rugs	76	78	93	91
Electrometallurgical Products	74	74	90	90
Medicinals and Botanicals	74	59	81	75
Household Refrigerators and Freezers	73	85	94	98
Metal Cans	73	66	84	79
Mineral Wool	71	75	84	89
Electron Tubes (Transmitting)	70	55	87	80

(Continued)

d. The government witholds these data to avoid disclosing information about individual companies.

Source: *1967 and 1972 Census of Manufacturers: Concentration Ratios in Manufacturing,* Washington, D.C.: Department of Commerce, Bureau of the Census.

Soap and Other Detergents	70	62	78	74
Photographic Equipment and Supplies	69	74	81	85
Cutlery	69	55	77	67
Explosives	67	67	91	86
Greeting Card Publishing	67	70	79	78
Beet Sugar	66	66	96	96
Transformers	65	59	78	75
Thread Mills	62	62	81	77
X-Ray Apparatus and Tubes	62	54	77	75
Storage Batteries	61	57	83	85
Glass Containers	60	55	75	76
Primary Zinc	59	66	90	d
Phonograph Records	58	48	67	61
Soybean Oil Mills	55	54	76	69
Ball and Roller Bearings	54	53	73	73
Knitting Mills	54	52	71	67
Distilled Liquor (Except Brandy)	54	47	71	73
Ceramic Wall and Floor Tile	52	56	76	71
Commercial Laundry Equipment	51	53	63	65
Radio and TV Receiving Sets	49	49	69	71
Sanitary Food Containers	49	46	68	64
Printing Ink	49	39	64	54
Wines, Brandy, and Brandy Spirits	48	53	63	68
Motors and Generators	48	47	60	59
Abrasive Products	48	49	57	60
Pulp Mills	45	59	70	83
Cheese	44	42	51	53
Raw Cane Sugar	43	44	65	62
Cottonseed Oil Mills	42	43	60	61
Copper Rolling and Drawing	41	39	65	61
Metal Office Furniture	38	42	52	54
Lime	35	37	54	53

growing importance of offshore production. Drilling on the Outer Continental Shelf is difficult and expensive and, for this reason, beyond the capabilities of many small companies. This trend may also reflect the diminishing importance of prorationing. The larger companies tend to have larger fields and, when prorationing was in effect, were more severely restricted in their production.

In short, the evidence does not indicate that the energy industries are highly concentrated. To the contrary, it suggests that these industries are among the least concentrated in the United States. Based on concentration ratios alone, there would seem to be little reason to worry about the anticompetitive behavior of the oil industry.

This conclusion is shared by others who have studied the industry's market structure. Duchesneau, in what is perhaps the most thorough study of concentration in the energy industries, also finds concentration levels to be relatively low.[2] However, concentration levels, by themselves, do not prove or disprove the existence of a competitive industry. Critics of the industry often admit that concentration levels are relatively low, but argue that anticompetitive behavior is manifested in other ways such as through vertical integration and joint ventures. Before considering these other issues, however, we first examine a special form of alleged concentration in the marketplace which has occupied a substantial amount of the time of the Congress and the Federal Energy Administration during the past two years—the argument that the major oil companies are increasing their share of the market for gasoline.

---

2. Duchesneau, Thomas D. *Competition in the U.S. Energy Industry.* Cambridge, Mass.: Ballinger Publishing Company, 1975. Chapter 2.

CHAPTER TWO

Market Shares in The Sale of Gasoline

One charge that has been leveled against the major oil companies in recent years is that they have expanded their share of the marketplace for refined products, especially gasoline, at the expense of independent marketers. Responding to this criticism, the Congress has required the President to issue monthly reports on gasoline market shares. The market shares issue has been a source of seemingly endless confusion. Critics of the oil industry have claimed that the major oil companies are driving independents from the market, that they are dominating the market in particular regions of the country, and that this is good reason for additional regulation of the large oil companies. To the contrary, we conclude that:

— There are many definitions of the word "independent," with the result that the discussion of the problems of the independents has been hopelessly confused.

— Using most definitions of "independent," there is no significant trend in the independent oil companies' share of motor gasoline sales between 1970 and 1974. If anything, gasoline sales have become less, rather than more, concentrated in the hands of the major integrated oil companies.

— There is no substance to the charge that major oil companies are withdrawing from some market areas and increasing their market share in other areas in order to dominate particular regions.

— Based on an analysis of market shares, the retail marketing of gasoline appears highly competitive.

In its preliminary report on the petroleum industry the Federal Trade Commission concluded that, "There can be little doubt that the independent sector of the petroleum industry, especially at the marketing level, has suffered most as a result of the present gasoline shortage."[1] Similarly, the Center for Science in the Public Interest, a public interest group, has charged that, "The major oil companies have tended to concentrate their power in recent years through the acquisition of other oil and fuel companies. The major oil companies have undertaken a policy of concentrating their market areas in certain geographic regions and of disposing of their stations in other areas."[2]

Allvine and Patterson attempt to show how the majors have been able to squeeze independents out of gasoline markets.[3] They discuss various factors which, they believe, have enabled the majors to increase their market shares, such as industry concentration, cartelization of crude production, federal tax breaks, and the import quota system. They also claim that the majors have effected this squeeze in other ways. These include underinvestment in new refinery capacity, underutilization of existing refinery capacity, withdrawal of the independents' supply, and the use of flashy and expensive marketing techniques.

Significantly, Allvine and Patterson never attempt to demonstrate whether the squeeze on the independents by the majors has actually taken place. In this section, we present data that suggest, in fact, that there has been little or no squeeze. The Allvine-Patterson argument is discussed at greater length in Chapter Four.

Even prior to the Arab oil embargo in 1973, protecting the independents' market share of gasoline sales had emerged as a major policy issue. This issue was not without some basis. The independent sector had been a highly competitive force in marketing refined products, especially gasoline. There was genuine concern in 1973 that the major oil companies might use a developing scarcity of gasoline and other refined products as a way of consolidating markets and raising prices. Also, some independent marketers had come to depend on purchases in the spot market at advantageous prices. As shortages began to appear, the spot market disappeared and the continued existence of this group of independent

1. U.S. Senate, Committee on Government Operations, *Preliminary Federal Trade Commission Staff Report on Its Investigation of the Petroleum Industry,* 93d Cong., 1st Sess., Comm. Print, 1973, p. 2.

2. Fritsch, A.J. and Egan, John W. *Big Oil: A Citizen's Factbook on the Major Oil Companies.* Center for Science in the Public Interest, 1973, p. 59.

3. Allvine, Fred C. and Paterson, James M. *Highway Robbery: An Analysis of the Gasoline Crisis.* Bloomington, Indiana: Indiana University Press, 1974.

marketers was threatened.[4]

On its surface the issue does not appear too complex. Either independents are being forced out of the marketplace or they are not. All that would seem to be needed is to examine the facts. However, analysis of this issue has never really progressed beyond a debate over the proper definition of the term "independent."

What is an independent? The oil industry is highly integrated; the 20 largest oil companies all own production, refining, and distribution facilities. If one were to define an independent on the basis of market share, which sector of the industry should be examined—crude oil sales, refinery sales, or product marketing? And, when independent crude oil producers sell to major refiners who, in turn, sell to independent gasoline dealers, the problem becomes even more complex. Under these conditions, it is not surprising that there are many possible definitions of the term "independent."

Independent refiners can be classified by control over crude production and, therefore, refinery input; size of total refinery capacity; size of individual refineries; or control over product. Developing an objective classification is difficult; some "independent" refiners operating small refineries could be defined as majors with respect to their crude supplies.

Distribution of gasoline and its retail sale is even more complex. Eighty-five percent of the nation's retail service stations are privately owned and operated. Some independents sell gasoline under a brand name; some do not. There are also branded and nonbranded company-owned stations. There are independent and company paid jobbers (wholesale gasoline distributors), some of whom sell branded gasoline as well as nonbranded gasoline. Obviously an assessment of the independents' market share has little meaning unless the term "independent" is agreed to and clearly defined from the start.

Adding to the confusion has been disagreement over the status of major oil company lessees. Most gasoline stations, including many stations selling under such widely recognized major brand names as Exxon, Shell, and Mobil are actually operated by independent oilmen not employed by the major oil companies. Many of these stations are

---

4. This is what triggered the litigation that culminated in *Davis v. Crown Central Petroleum Corporation,* 483 F. 2d 1014 (4th Cir. 1973). As crude supplies tightened in early 1973, Crown Central, an independent refiner, stopped supplying its noncontract customers. Two independent marketers then sued Crown Central. The Court of Appeals dismissed the case, telling the independents to make their case to Congress. Three months after this decision was handed down the Emergency Petroleum Allocation Act was passed. See also *Mullis v. ARCO Petroleum Corp.,* 502 F.2d 290 (7th Cir. 1974).

also owned by their independent operators. However, in some cases, the real estate and equipment of the independently run major brand stations is owned by the major oil company and leased to the operators. A best guess is that roughly 30 percent of all gasoline stations fall into this category.

Lessee operators are no more employees of the major oil companies than a person who rents an apartment is an employee of the apartment owner. Rather, they are independent businessmen who, for one reason or another, have chosen to rent rather than purchase their facilities. However, some critics of the industry have charged that their independence is illusory; because they rent their premises and equipment they are, in effect, controlled by the major oil companies. For this reason, the majors' dominance of marketing is far greater than statistics on salary-operated stations would suggest. FEA has classified lessees as independents. We see no compelling reason to disagree.

The Emergency Petroleum Allocation Act of 1973 charged the government with preserving the independent marketers' share of gasoline sales. In addition, the government is required to report monthly changes in the independents' market share. During the early months of the Arab oil embargo, the Federal Energy office was too preoccupied to pay much attention to these provisions. Finally, in April 1974, Temple, Barker and Sloane, a consulting firm commissioned to study market shares in gasoline sales, found that the independents' market share had fallen sharply since the previous year.[5] However, two basic errors were made in this study. First, it defined independents as marketers not selling under a major brand name rather than as owners and operators of service stations as defined by the law. The definition used by the study was, if anything, more applicable to the crude oil allocaton program than to the gasoline allocation program. In addition, the consultant's study combined two disparate sets of data, the second, more recent set clearly being faulty.[6] As a result, the study's conclusion, that the non-major market share had fallen from 29 percent in 1972 to 19 percent in April 1974, was incorrect. Copies of the report were withheld by FEA because of the study's shortcomings. Subsequently, all outstanding copies were ordered destroyed by then acting FEO

---

5. Temple, Barker & Sloane, Inc. "An Evaluation of Alternative FEO Allocation Programs on Motor Gasoline Markets and Marketers," April 11, 1974.

6. In particular, it combined Lundberg Survey data prior to December 1973 with data generated by the Federal Energy Office and compiled by TBS after December. The apparent sharp reduction in market shares for independents, suggested by the TBS survey, occurred at the time of the break in data. We are especially indebted to Daniel Lundberg for assistance in using and interpreting the Lundberg Survey data in this and the following chapter.

Administrator John Sawhill. Nonetheless, rumors that an FEO study had found that the independents' market share had been seriously eroded leaked to the public, lending substance to similar charges made by certain independent marketers.

We present in Table 4 three additional series based on three separate definitions of "independent."[7] One is a corrected version of the Temple, Barker and Sloane survey based on one consistent set of data—the Lundberg Survey.[8] With hindsight, and using the TBS definition of "independent," there would appear to have been, if anything, a slight increase in the independents' market share between 1972 and 1974.

The second series presented in Table 4, also based on the Lundberg data, assumes the definition implicit in the Federal Trade Commission's current investigation of the eight largest major oil companies.[9] Using this definition, it would again appear that, if anything, the market share of the independents has increased slightly over time.

The third set of data on market shares, presented in Table 4, assumes the definition of "independent" used in the Lundberg Survey. This survey is the only continuous source of data on gasoline sales by company readily available to the public. Lundberg has been publishing his own survey of market shares for a number of years. This survey indicates a persistent increase in the non-majors' share of the market since 1970. Unfortunately, Lundberg's data do not correspond to the definition of independent or non-major used by FEA or adopted by the Congress in the Emergency Petroleum Allocation Act. Once again, these data are based on brand name rather than on ownership and operation of station.[10]

For this reason, the Federal Energy Administration commissioned

---

7. These series are based on the Lundberg data which are, in turn, based on state tax receipts. Sometimes major distributors will pay the tax and than resell gasoline to non-branded retailers. This poses a problem for someone attempting to assign market shares between "majors" and "independents" using the Lundberg data.

8. The TBS survey defines a major marketer as a distributor selling under the name of a refiner having 175,000 bpd or more of refinery capacity. According to the TBS report, this includes: Phillips, Sun, Union, Sohio, Citgo, Conoco, Marathon, Ashland, Hess, and American Petrofina. All others are defined as nonmajors. The FEA has now repudiated this definition.

9. The FTC is investigating the eight largest oil companies: Exxon, Texaco, Gulf, Mobil, Chevron, Amoco, Shell and Arco. Therefore, the FTC definition of a non-major, used here, is the share of gasoline sales by companies selling under names other than those listed above.

10. In particular, Lundberg defines a non-major as any gasoline retailer not flying the Exxon, Texaco, Shell, Mobil, Gulf, Amoco, Chevron, Arco, Sun, Phillips, Union, Conoco, Citgo, Ashland, Marathon, Sohio, Tenneco, Getty, BP Oil, or Skelly flag. This definition reflects the needs and interests of Lundberg's subscribers.

TABLE 4

RETAIL SALES OF GASOLINE BY NON-MAJOR OIL COMPANIES
(PERCENT OF TOTAL SALES)

ANNUAL

Date	TBS Definition	FTC Definition	Conventional Lundberg Definition
1970	23.8	45.4	22.6
1971	25.7	47.2	24.4
1972	27.4	48.4	26.7
1973	27.2	47.6	26.7
1974	27.8	48.2	26.4
(Jan.-June)			

MONTHLY

1973

	TBS Definition	FTC Definition	Conventional Lundberg Definition
Jan.	28.4	49.4	26.8
Feb.	28.4	49.5	26.7
Mar.	27.7	48.4	26.1
Apr.	27.6	48.1	25.9
May	26.1	46.1	24.4
June	26.2	46.5	24.7
July	26.2	46.4	25.2
Aug.	26.0	46.2	25.1
Sept.	27.1	47.5	26.3
Oct.	27.3	48.0	26.4
Nov.	27.2	48.0	26.3
Dec.	28.6	49.4	27.3

1974

	TBS Definition	FTC Definition	Conventional Lundberg Definition
Jan.	27.8	48.7	26.6
Feb.	28.5	49.0	27.0
Mar.	27.9	48.6	26.7
Apr.	28.8	48.3	27.0
May	27.2	47.6	25.9
June	26.7	46.7	25.4

Source: All calculations of market shares are based on the *Lundberg Survey of the Gasoline Market*, 1970 to 1974.

13

TABLE 5

PERCENTAGE SHARE OF THE GASOLINE MARKET BY TYPES OF MARKETERS AS REPORTED BY LUNDBERG SURVEY, INC.

	Branded Independents	Nonbranded Independents	Total Independents	Total All Other
1972				
Jan.	75.93	9.72	85.65	14.35
Feb.	76.25	9.54	85.79	14.21
Mar.	75.85	9.71	85.56	14.44
Apr.	75.38	10.20	85.58	14.42
May	74.97	10.20	85.17	14.83
June	75.08	10.01	85.09	14.91
July	75.35	10.01	85.36	14.64
Aug.	74.91	9.89	84.80	15.20
Sept.	74.63	10.27	84.90	15.10
Oct.	73.05	10.78	83.83	16.17
Nov.	74.24	10.87	85.11	14.89
Dec.	74.02	10.88	84.90	15.10
Total:	74.95	10.18	85.13	14.87
1973				
Jan.	73.59	11.71	85.30	14.70
Feb.	73.89	11.82	85.71	14.29
Mar.	74.56	10.65	85.21	14.79
Apr.	75.47	10.43	85.90	14.10
May	75.32	9.78	85.10	14.90
June	75.12	10.53	85.65	14.35
July	75.54	9.86	85.40	14.60
Aug.	75.76	9.76	85.52	14.48
Sept.	74.33	10.49	84.82	15.18
Oct.	74.66	10.43	85.09	14.91
Nov.	74.56	10.89	85.45	14.55
Dec.	73.90	11.15	85.05	14.95
Total	74.71	10.59	85.30	14.70

(Continued)

14

1974

Jan.	74.18	10.86	85.04	14.96
Feb.	73.49	11.53	85.02	14.98
Preliminary:				
Mar.	73.05	11.57	84.62	15.38
Apr.	73.43	11.33	84.76	15.24

Source: Federal Energy Administration, *Petroleum Market Shares: A Progress Report on the Retailing of Gasoline*. Washington, D.C.: U.S. Government Printing Office, August 6, 1974, p.7.

Lundberg to rework his data to develop a series on market shares consistent with the definition of "independent" contained in the Emergency Petroleum Allocation Act.[11] The results, reproduced in Table 5, suggest that the share of all independents remained more or less constant between January 1972 and April 1974, with a slight decrease in the share of branded independents and a corresponding increase in the share of nonbranded independents.[12] There would appear to be little justification for the charge that the independent marketers have been squeezed out of business by the major oil companies.

In June 1974, the Independent Gasoline Marketers' Council made public its own study of market shares in the form of a press release. This study purported to show that the market share of independent nonbranded marketers had fallen sharply between the first quarter of 1972 and the first quarter of 1974.[13] Based on data supplied by IGMC members, it found that the gasoline sales of independents

---

11. The revised Lundberg study is discussed in Federal Energy Administration, *Petroleum Market Shares: A Progress Report on the Retailing of Gasoline*. Washington, D.C.: U.S. Government Printing Office, August 6, 1974, pp. 3-8.

12. The Lundberg data are based on state gasoline tax records which, by themselves, do not indicate gasoline sales to final consumers by the categories of retailers specified in the Act. Lundberg recognized this problem and tried to adjust for it.

13. FEA. *Petroleum Market Shares*, p. 9; *Oil and Gas Journal*. March 24, 1975, p. 39.

had fallen 17.1 percent while total industry sales rose 0.3 percent during the two-year period.

The major problem with this survey is that the IGMC is not representative of all nonbranded independent marketers, even though on some occasions it has claimed to speak for this segment of the industry.[14] It consists of 15 of the larger nonbranded independent marketers of gasoline. These marketers account for only 16 percent of the total volume sold through nonbranded independent outlets and less than 2 percent of total gasoline sales. The IGMC also consists of marketers who, when gasoline was in excess supply, generally purchased large volumes on the spot market at distress prices. By contrast, many other marketers, including many nonbranded independents, chose to purchase much of their gasoline from refiners under contract. Others purchased without benefit of long-term contracts but from the same refiners over long periods of time and, in this way, built up good will and satisfactory relations with their suppliers. Although gasoline purchased under these conditions cost more, the buyer was supposedly protected against shortages such as those that occurred in 1973-1974. In short, marketers who purchased heavily on the spot market and did not establish good relations with their suppliers took a high risk gamble, made abnormal profits as long as there were surpluses of gasoline, but then began to hurt when this gamble turned sour. For this reason, it is not surprising that the IGMC marketers lost their share of the market between 1972 and 1974.

In July 1974, Lewin & Associates, Inc. conducted a "quick survey" of nonbranded gasoline stations for FEA.[15] This survey concentrated on the larger nonbranded independent gasoline marketers, including all 15 members of the Independent Gasoline Marketers' Council. A total of 56 companies responded to the survey. The results indicated that, during the first four months of 1974, the independents in the sample had experienced a decline in market share of 14.8 percent since the first four months of 1972.

The Lewin survey was stratified into two groups: marketers with monthly sales over 3 million gallons and marketers with monthly sales of less than 3 million gallons. The Lewin sample consisted, for the most part, of the same types of independent marketers included in the IGMC survey—nonbranded marketers who have depended heavily on purchases in the spot market. For this reason, the Lewin

---

14. For example, see the testimony of Ken Catmull on behalf of the Independent Gasoline Marketers Council before the Subcommittee on Government Regulation, Senate Small Business Committee, August 20, 1974, reproduced in 120 *Cong. Rec.* S15432 (daily ed. August 21, 1974).

15. FEA. *Petroleum Market Shares: A Progress Report,* pp. 11-16.

survey suffers from the same biases as the IGMC survey and, because of these biases, gives the appearance of decline in the market share of all independents during the two-year period.

Because of this confusion of statistical sources, the Federal Energy Administration decided to undertake its own study of market shares.[16] The FEA survey adopted as the most appropriate definition of "independent" sales through outlets not owned and operated by the company producing the gasoline.

The results are presented in Table 6. The FEA survey found that during the first five months of 1974 gasoline sales by branded and nonbranded independent marketers were 82.7 percent of total sales, compared to 83.4 percent during the first five months of 1972. During the same period, however, the large integrated refiners', or major oil companies', share of gasoline sales through all outlets fell from 74.8 percent to 73.7 percent of the total, with a comparable increase in the small and independent refiners' share of gasoline sales. In general, FEA's survey suggested very little change in market shares during the period.[17] If the independent marketers were being squeezed, they were being squeezed by the independent refiners and not the integrated oil companies.

What has happened since mid-1974? On March 4, 1975, FEA issued its first monthly market shares report as required by the Emergency Petroleum Allocation Act. This report was for October and November 1974. The most recently issued report available at the time this book was completed carries the series to May 1975.[18] These monthly reports are based on a continuous sample of 10,000 stations conducted by the Census Bureau. They divide gasoline marketers into three groups: nonbranded independents; branded independents; and refiner/marketers. FEA's newly created series suggests that, for the eight months covered by the data, the market shares of nonbranded independents and refiner/marketers have increased, while the share of branded independents has decreased. (See Table 7.)

FEA has warned users, correctly, that seasonal variations in market shares should not be confused with long-term trends.[19] As a rule, one would expect the share of branded outlets to peak during the summer months, when tourism is greatest, and to fall during the

---

16. Federal Energy Administration. *Petroleum Market Shares: A Report on the Federal Energy Administration Survey of Refiners and Importers of Gasoline.* Washington, D.C.: August 28, 1974.

17. The maximum decline in the independent marketers' share occurred between July 1972 and January 1974. This was 4.2 percent, far lower than the IGMC and Lewin estimates.

18. FEA. *Petroleum Market Shares,* May 1975, p. 5.

19. *Petroleum Market Shares.* January 4, 1975, p. 3.

TABLE 6

FEA SURVEY OF REFINERS AND IMPORTERS OF GASOLINE
(PERCENT)

Total Sales Through:

Month	Retail Outlets Owned and Operated by Integrated Oil Companies	Other Direct Sales by the Integrated Companies	Branded and Nonbranded Independent Marketers
1972			
Jan.	8.17	8.43	83.40
Feb.	7.81	8.65	83.55
Mar.	7.91	8.66	83.43
Apr.	8.09	8.33	83.57
May	7.65	9.12	83.23
June	7.74	8.37	83.88
July	8.22	6.62	85.16
Aug.	7.88	8.26	83.87
Sept.	7.96	8.23	83.81
Oct.	7.89	8.87	83.25
Nov.	8.02	8.41	83.58
Dec.	9.20	8.02	82.77
1973			
Jan.	8.33	8.08	83.59
Feb.	8.26	8.03	83.71
Mar.	8.12	8.02	83.86
Apr.	8.00	7.99	84.01
May	8.09	8.55	83.36
June	8.75	7.93	83.32
July	8.96	7.29	83.74
Aug.	8.80	7.69	83.52
Sept.	9.37	7.65	82.98
Oct.	9.40	8.28	82.32
Nov.	9.69	8.32	81.98
Dec.	9.81	7.73	82.46

(Continued)

18

1974

Jan.	10.06	8.37	81.57
Feb.	9.16	8.40	82.45
Mar.	8.83	8.51	82.66
Apr.	8.54	8.24	83.22
May	8.32	8.38	83.30

Source: Federal Energy Administration, *Petroleum Market Shares: A Report on the Federal Energy Administration Survey of Refiners and Importers of Gasoline,* Washington, D.C.: U.S. Government Printing Office, August 28, 1974, p. 24.

non-summer months, when tourism is off. Tourists away from home tend to favor nationally known, branded stations accepting credit cards.

FEA's series still failed to silence complaints by some independent marketers of gasoline that their shares were being eroded.[20] For this reason, in 1975 FEA conducted another historical survey of the independent gasoline distributors' market shares.[21] In this survey FEA collected information on gasoline sales from over 300 nonbranded independent marketers. These were defined as marketers having no refining capacity of their own, not controlled by refiners, not leasing their premises from refiners, and not selling under refiner brand names. The more than 300 companies in the sample accounted for about two-thirds of gasoline sales by independent nonbranded marketers.

FEA's latest survey uses the most restrictive definition of the word "independent" yet adopted by the government. It attempts to

---

20. *Oil and Gas Journal.* March 24, 1975, p. 39.

21. This survey was completed in the autumn of 1975 but has not yet been released. Draft copies have been circulated under the title, *Historical Report on Nonbranded Independent Marketers of Motor Gasoline: 1972 through 1974.*

TABLE 7

MARKET SHARES OF GASOLINE SERVICE STATION
OPERATORS
1974-1975

(PERCENTAGE)

Month	Refiner/ Marketers	Nonbranded Independents	Branded Independents
October 1974	13.3	7.4	79.3
November 1974	13.5	8.3	78.2
December 1974	14.0	9.0	76.9
January 1975	15.3	9.1	75.6
February 1975	14.5	9.6	75.9
March 1975	15.1	9.6	75.3
April 1975	14.6	10.2	75.2
May 1975*	14.3	9.9	75.8

*Preliminary

Source: Federal Energy Administration. National Energy Information Center, *Petroleum Market Shares,* May 1975, p. 5.

measure the market share of the "true" independent, the group of marketers including the IGMC membership. It excludes all major company lessees.

The results of FEA's latest survey are summarized in Table 8. In 1973 and early 1974, the market share of the sample firms fell from about 5.2 percent to about 4.5 percent of total gasoline sales. This was during a period of crude oil and product shortages. As one might expect, these shortages hit hardest the nonbranded segment of the industry. However, by the fourth quarter of 1974 the nonbranded independent marketers had more than restored their 1972 market shares. By then, they accounted for 5.5 percent of total gasoline sales.

This restoration of market shares might reflect the establishment of the mandatory allocation program in early 1974. More likely, it reflects the restoration of surplus production and a spot market for gasoline. Increasingly, the shortages of 1973-74 appear to have been an aberration in what has been a prevailing tendency toward excess production of gasoline and penetration of marketing by independent, nonbranded operators.

Critics of FEA's surveys have argued that they are misleading

TABLE 8

RESULTS OF FEA'S 1975 SURVEY
OF SELECTED INDEPENDENT NONBRANDED MARKETERS OF GASOLINE

(Percentage of total U.S. gasoline sales)

1972 through 1974

1972	1st quarter	4.96
	2nd quarter	4.98
	3rd quarter	5.14
	4th quarter	5.43
	Annual	5.13
1973	1st quarter	5.22
	2nd quarter	4.31
	3rd quarter	4.08
	4th quarter	4.29
	Annual	4.46
1974	1st quarter	4.42
	2nd quarter	4.59
	3rd quarter	4.85
	4th quarter	5.51
	Annual	4.86

Source: Computed from Federal Energy Administration, *Historical Report on Nonbranded Independent Marketers of Motor Gasoline, 1972 through 1974*, draft report, 1975, Table 1.

because the major oil companies have withdrawn the privilege of using their trademarks from many branded independent jobbers and distributors, thus forcibly converting them from branded to nonbranded independents. In fact, there are relatively few cases of this happening and no evidence that it has happened on an increased scale sufficient to explain the shift in market shares indicated by FEA's latest surveys.[22] Rather, these surveys, if they reflect any

22. Based on discussions with a number of independent nonbranded marketers.

long-term trends, reflect the shift in public demand from branded dealers to cut-rate, self-service outlets owned and operated by both independents and major oil companies.[23] Increasingly, the public has been seeking bargains and, with the price spreads that have existed over the past year, some shift in market shares to nonbranded outlets has been inevitable.

Finally, it has been charged that some majors have changed their marketing operations, increasing their sales through secondary brands or nonbranded outlets. As a case in point, Exxon has been accused of driving some of its own independent branded stations from the market by selling lower priced gasoline under the name Alert, a marketing outlet entirely owned and operated by Exxon. However, to assume that this is monopolistic is to assume that Exxon's Alert stations have little or no competition from other companies selling at cut-rate prices. The growth in automated cut-rate service stations owned and operated by the major oil companies is primarily the result of competition from nonbranded retailers and the greater complexity of the automobile.[24] It is competitive, not monopolistic practices, that have resulted in greater direct marketing by the majors through secondary brand and self-service outlets.

In conclusion, FEA's data on market shares show that retail sales of gasoline are not dominated by the major oil companies. Even if the majors were to expand the number of their company-owned and operated outlets, they would have a long way to go before becoming the principal marketers of gasoline in the United States. Gasoline sales have been and remain an industry dominated by independents.

In short, the evidence does not support the view that the major oil companies, however they may be defined, should be subject to special regulations because of monopolistic tendencies in the marketing of gasoline. To the contrary, the evidence suggests competition in the marketing of gasoline and the presence of a vigorous and thriving independent segment of the industry.

---

23. For further discussion, see *Lundberg Letter,* October 24, 1975.

24. Because of EPA-mandated exhaust control and other types of equipment that are now standard on newer automobiles, it is increasingly difficult for the neighborhood service station to service automobiles. This has, in turn, encouraged volume sales of gasoline at discount prices as the principal means of competing in the industry.

CHAPTER THREE

Regional Concentration of Market Shares in the Sale of Gasoline

Some critics of the oil industry argue that data on national market shares are meaningless. In recent years, the major oil companies have been pulling out, or plan to pull out, of particular regions. Phillips is getting out of New England, Gulf out of the Rocky Mountain area. The result, it is argued, is greater concentration and diminished competition in the industry in certain regions of the country, if not in the country as a whole.

This argument can be reduced to the level of absurdity. Only one gasoline station can occupy a lot. By necessity, that station is a monopoly on that lot. One can, in other words, create monopoly by defining a region sufficiently small. Nevertheless, the argument that there is greater concentration in sales on a regional basis should be analyzed. To this end, we focus on the state. We also focus, once again, on sales of gasoline, the refined product in which market concentration has allegedly had the most serious anticompetitive consequences.

To do this, we have reworked data generated by the Lundberg Survey. Table 9 lists the top five gasoline marketers state-by-state in 1973 and compares their market shares with shares for the preceding three years. If the major oil companies are concentrating their gasoline sales in particular regions, data in Table 9 should indicate this. It does not.

TABLE 9
STATE-BY-STATE ANNUAL AVERAGE
RETAIL MARKET SHARES (1970 to 1973)
(percentage)

STATE	TOP FIVE MARKETERS (1973)	1970	1971	1972	1973	1970 to 1973 CHANGE IN PERCENTAGE POINTS
ALABAMA	KYSO	14.5	14.1	13.4	13.4	— 1.1
	GULF	9.5	8.9	6.7	9.1	— .4
	SHELL	8.0	7.6	7.5	8.1	+ .1
	TEXACO	6.7	6.6	6.8	6.9	+ .2
	TRIANGLE	6.4	6.3	6.0	5.8	— .6
ALASKA						
	SOCAL	55.3	49.0	41.4	39.2	—16.1
	TEXACO	16.4	17.4	17.6	13.9	— 2.5
	UNION	21.2	17.2	17.2	20.8	— 1.2
	TESORO	--	5.4	17.3	20.1	+ 20.1
ARIZONA						
	SOCAL	15.8	14.6	14.4	14.4	— 1.4
	SHELL	14.0	14.5	14.7	17.0	+ 3.0
	TEXACO	8.6	8.2	7.5	7.6	— 1.0
	EXXON	7.5	7.2	7.0	7.8	+ .3
	UNION	5.6	5.6	5.5	6.9	+ 1.3
ARKANSAS						
	EXXON	12.8	11.6	11.4	13.8	+ 1.0
	GULF	8.1	7.8	7.8	8.5	+ .4
	TEXACO	8.5	7.8	7.7	7.9	— .6
	MOBIL	7.2	6.3	6.7	6.7	— .5
	TOSCO	0	0	4.7	6.5	+ 6.5
CALIFORNIA						
	SOCAL	17.5	15.9	16.4	16.6	— .9
	SHELL	16.2	14.8	14.0	15.1	— 1.1
	ARCO	9.5	11.1	10.6	10.6	+ 1.1
	UNION	10.3	10.0	9.1	10.0	— .3
	MOBIL	9.4	9.1	8.9	8.6	— .8

(Continued)

24

COLORADO

CONOCO	11.4	10.9	10.7	12.3	+	.9
TEXACO	12.2	12.1	11.6	11.6	—	.6
AMOCO	9.1	9.6	9.2	9.6	+	.5
PHILLIPS	8.1	7.3	8.1	7.7	—	.4
CHEVRON	4.9	5.0	5.9	6.7	+	1.8

CONNECTICUT

MOBIL	14.0	14.2	14.1	14.4	—	.4
TEXACO	12.3	11.4	11.2	11.6	—	.7
SHELL	10.2	9.5	9.5	9.7	—	.5
EXXON	8.0	8.0	7.8	8.6	+	.6
AMOCO	8.1	8.2	8.9	8.6	+	.5

DELAWARE

EXXON	17.6	16.6	16.5	17.8	+	.2
ARCO	14.0	14.5	14.3	16.0	+	2.0
GULF	8.6	7.7	7.8	8.9	+	.3
GETTY	7.4	8.9	9.0	8.6	+	1.2
SUN	8.5	8.5	8.9	8.0	—	.5

DISTRICT OF COLUMBIA

EXXON	30.4	29.7	27.6	30.4		0
AMOCO	18.5	17.4	17.9	17.1	—	1.4
GULF	13.3	11.9	13.2	14.5	+	1.2
TEXACO	9.0	10.7	10.6	9.8	+	.8
SHELL	6.3	6.3	7.3	7.4	+	1.1

FLORIDA

KYSO	13.6	12.4	11.9	11.7	—	1.9
GULF	9.7	9.3	9.2	10.0	+	.3
SHELL	8.4	8.2	8.2	8.6	+	.2
TEXACO	7.6	7.4	7.2	7.3	—	.3
AMOCO	7.3	7.0	7.3	7.0	+	.3

GEORGIA

GULF	11.8	11.2	11.8	12.4	+	.6
CHEVRON	14.1	13.4	12.4	12.3	—	1.8
TEXACO	7.7	7.3	7.4	7.4	—	.3
AMOCO	7.2	7.3	7.2	6.7	—	.5
SHELL	7.1	6.5	6.2	6.6	—	.5

(Continued)

25

HAWAII

SOCAL	37.0	35.6	30.1	32.0	— 5.0
SHELL	19.4	18.6	28.4	28.4	+ 9.0
UNION	18.5	18.3	16.7	16.8	— 1.7
PHILLIPS	12.2	12.3	11.0	10.5	— 1.7
TEXACO	9.0	9.5	8.2	7.6	— 1.4

IDAHO

PHILLIPS	9.7	10.3	11.1	9.9	+ 1.2
CONOCO	9.7	9.3	8.9	9.7	0
AMOCO	8.1	8.7	9.0	8.9	+ .8
TEXACO	9.2	8.6	7.8	8.2	— 1.0
CHEVRON	—	6.0	5.7	6.3	6.3

ILLINOIS

AMOCO	20.0	19.4	19.3	19.1	— .9
SHELL	10.5	10.2	10.2	10.7	+ .2
CLARK	5.4	5.5	6.0	6.8	+ 1.4
TEXACO	6.4	6.9	6.8	6.3	— .1
MOBIL	5.8	5.5	5.7	5.6	— .2

INDIANA

AMOCO	15.0	14.0	13.9	14.1	— .9
SHELL	10.2	9.3	8.8	9.1	— 1.1
MARATHON	10.1	10.7	8.7	8.3	— 1.8
PHILLIPS	4.3	4.5	4.6	7.4	+ 3.1
SUN	7.2	7.0	6.1	6.2	— 1.0

IOWA

AMOCO	17.5	17.2	17.0	18.4	+ .9
SUN	8.8	8.6	9.2	9.8	+ 1.0
PHILLIPS	6.2	6.0	6.3	6.0	— .2
CONOCO	3.7	3.8	4.0	4.4	+ .6
MOBIL	3.7	4.1	4.0	4.2	+ .5

KANSAS

AMOCO	10.6	10.3	11.0	11.9	+ 1.3
VICKERS	7.0	6.9	6.9	7.2	+ .2
PHILLIPS	8.6	8.5	7.5	7.0	— 1.6
MOBIL	6.7	6.7	6.2	6.4	— .3
DERBY	5.8	6.1	5.4	5.6	— .2

(Continued)

KENTUCKY

KYSO	18.2	17.2	16.6	16.4	—	1.8
ASHLAND	15.3	14.8	14.3	15.6	+	.3
GULF	10.6	10.0	9.9	10.2	—	.4
SHELL	6.9	6.7	7.0	7.2	+	.3
TEXACO	8.0	7.9	7.5	6.9	—	1.1

LOUISIANA

EXXON	15.7	18.5	19.8	17.5	+	1.8
GULF	10.4	10.6	10.7	10.2	—	.2
CONOCO	9.6	9.3	8.2	8.0	—	1.6
TEXACO	11.9	12.0	10.8	7.3	—	4.6
SHELL	6.6	7.1	7.6	5.9	—	.7

MAINE

EXXON	13.3	12.9	12.0	13.7	+	.4
MOBIL	12.1	11.3	10.8	11.2	—	.9
GULF	10.2	9.6	9.7	11.1	+	.9
TEXACO	10.1	10.2	9.9	10.0	—	.1
BP OIL	6.2	9.8	11.4	9.4	+	3.2

MARYLAND

EXXON	18.7	17.6	17.4	19.3	+	.7
AMOCO	9.9	9.9	10.3	9.8	—	.1
SHELL	9.0	8.6	9.1	8.7	—	.3
GULF	7.4	6.9	7.6	7.9	+	.5
TEXACO	7.6	7.4	8.2	6.4	—	1.2

MASSACHUSETTS

MOBIL	13.8	13.6	14.1	14.9	+	1.1
TEXACO	9.6	9.7	9.6	9.7	+	.1
SHELL	9.1	8.9	9.0	9.1		0
BP OIL	9.3	10.2	10.1	9.0	—	.3
EXXON	7.8	7.5	7.3	8.2	+	.4

MICHIGAN

AMOCO	17.2	15.4	14.6	14.5	—	2.7
SHELL	11.4	9.9	10.2	10.2	—	1.2
MOBIL	9.5	9.2	8.5	8.1	—	1.4
SUN	6.1	6.2	6.3	6.2	+	.1
GULF	8.0	7.2	6.5	6.1	—	1.9

(Continued)

MINNESOTA

AMOCO	15.2	16.0	16.5	16.3	+	1.1
NORTH-WESTERN	6.9	6.9	8.1	9.0	+	2.1
MOBIL	7.0	7.3	8.4	8.5	+	1.5
PHILLIPS	6.6	6.5	6.4	6.5	—	.1
CONOCO	5.6	5.1	5.1	5.6		0

MISSISSIPPI

KYSO	13.1	12.3	13.2	13.2	+	.1
GULF	9.4	8.4	9.5	9.5	+	.1
EXXON	5.0	5.8	6.6	7.2	+	2.2
TEXACO	7.8	7.4	7.3	7.3	—	.6
SEAGO ENTR	--	--	1.1	6.0	+	6.0

MISSOURI

AMOCO	15.9	15.0	15.1	14.6	—	1.3
PHILLIPS	10.1	9.2	8.7	8.4	—	1.7
SHELL	6.2	5.7	5.4	5.7	—	.5
MOBIL	5.7	5.0	4.6	5.1	—	.6
TEXACO	4.7	4.7	4.2	4.5	—	.2

MONTANA

CONOCO	15.1	14.4	14.4	15.1		0
TEXACO	13.4	13.3	13.6	12.7	—	.7
CENEX	11.0	9.9	9.7	10.3	—	.7
AMOCO	10.4	10.5	10.2	10.1	—	.3
EXXON	10.9	9.9	9.2	9.6	—	1.3

NEBRASKA

AMOCO	10.7	11.3	11.8	12.2	+	1.5
PHILLIPS	10.6	10.2	9.2	9.8	—	.8
FARMLAND	9.5	9.1	8.5	8.9	—	.6
MOBIL	8.9	8.7	8.4	8.9		0
CONOCO	7.9	7.6	7.3	7.9		0

(Continued)

NEVADA

SOCAL	19.4	17.8	17.8	17.3	—	2.1
PHILLIPS	11.3	11.6	11.9	14.2	+	2.9
SHELL	12.2	10.7	10.0	11.2	—	1.0
ARCO	7.7	7.9	9.7	8.8	+	1.1
UNION	6.5	6.5	6.1	7.8	+	1.3

NEW HAMPSHIRE

MOBIL	13.1	11.8	11.5	12.4	—	.7
TEXACO	9.9	10.3	10.0	10.1	+	.2
GULF	10.0	8.7	8.4	9.7	—	.3
EXXON	9.5	9.1	8.4	9.2	—	.3
SHELL	9.1	8.5	8.4	8.9	—	.2

NEW JERSEY

EXXON	18.7	17.8	16.7	19.4	+	.7
SUN	9.5	9.2	9.2	8.8	—	.7
HESS	7.5	9.2	9.3	8.6	+	1.1
GULF	8.0	6.4	7.2	7.6	—	.4
SHELL	7.5	7.2	6.9	7.0	—	.5

NEW MEXICO

TEXACO	12.2	12.2	13.2	12.5	+	.3
CHEVRON	13.8	12.6	12.3	12.2	—	1.4
PHILLIPS	8.4	8.3	8.2	7.6	—	.8
SHELL	7.5	7.4	7.7	7.5		0
EXXON	6.4	6.8	5.8	6.3	—	.1

NEW YORK

MOBIL	19.8	18.7	18.7	19.1	—	.7
TEXACO	10.7	11.0	11.1	10.3	—	.4
SHELL	9.9	8.9	9.1	9.1	—	.8
EXXON	9.1	8.6	9.0	9.0	—	.1
GULF	8.4	6.9	7.6	7.6	—	.8

NORTH CAROLINA

EXXON	15.4	12.6	14.5	16.8	+	1.4
GULF	9.4	9.6	8.0	9.0	—	.4
TEXACO	8.5	9.2	7.8	8.8	+	.3
SHELL	7.1	6.8	6.5	6.8	—	.3
AMOCO	7.5	7.5	6.5	5.8	—	1.7

(Continued)

NORTH DAKOTA

AMOCO	27.4	27.1	26.7	27.2	—	.2
CENEX	17.9	17.9	17.3	18.1	—	.2
MOBIL	12.1	12.3	11.8	10.3	—	1.8
TEXACO	6.6	6.8	6.8	6.9	+	.3
PHILLIPS	3.5	3.6	3.8	4.5	+	1.0

OHIO

SOHIO	27.6	26.5	24.7	24.9	—	2.7
MARATHON	8.6	8.8	7.6	7.6	—	1.0
ASHLAND	6.9	7.3	7.8	7.4	+	.5
SHELL	8.0	7.5	7.5	7.2	—	.8
SUN	9.0	8.3	7.8	7.1	—	1.9

OKLAHOMA

TEXACO	9.9	10.4	10.8	12.2	+	2.3
PHILLIPS	10.9	10.5	9.7	9.6	—	1.3
CONOCO	9.0	9.0	9.0	8.9	—	.1
CHAMPLIN	6.1	7.0	7.3	7.5	+	1.4
SUN	7.6	7.5	7.1	7.2	—	.4

OREGON

ARCO	14.0	15.4	15.9	16.4	+	2.4
SOCAL	15.8	14.6	13.9	14.7	—	1.1
SHELL	12.1	11.0	10.8	11.7	—	.4
TEXACO	9.1	9.8	10.2	11.0	—	1.9
UNION	9.6	9.0	8.2	8.5	—	1.1

PENNSYLVANIA

ARCO	16.9	16.7	15.8	16.8	—	.1
EXXON	12.5	11.2	10.7	12.6	+	.1
SUN	10.5	10.5	10.2	9.9	+	.6
GULF	8.9	8.2	8.2	9.1	+	.2
TEXACO	7.5	8.0	7.9	8.1	+	.6

RHODE ISLAND

MOBIL	12.7	12.7	11.7	12.3	—	.4
TEXACO	11.2	10.3	8.2	11.8	—	.6
BP OIL	9.3	6.2	14.4	10.2	—	.9
GULF	10.5	10.0	9.5	9.1	—	1.4
SHELL	8.4	8.1	8.3	9.0	+	.6

(Continued)

SOUTH CAROLINA

EXXON	16.2	16.2	16.2	18.2	+	2.0
GULF	13.6	11.9	11.1	11.6	—	2.0
SHELL	9.6	8.8	8.6	8.8	—	.8
TEXACO	8.8	8.6	7.8	7.8	—	1.0
AMOCO	6.4	6.2	6.1	6.0	—	.4

SOUTH DAKOTA

AMOCO	18.9	18.9	20.5	20.9	+	2.0
MOBIL	12.8	12.1	10.9	11.5	—	1.3
CENEX	8.6	8.4	8.0	7.9	—	.7
TEXACO	6.6	6.8	5.6	6.8	+	.2
COOPS	5.4	5.4	5.5	5.6	+	.2

TENNESSEE

EXXON	15.5	14.4	13.4	15.4	—	..1
GULF	10.3	9.3	9.5	9.3	—	1.0
AMOCO	8.0	7.8	7.7	7.6	—	.4
SHELL	8.0	7.6	7.4	7.2	—	.8
CITGO	7.7	8.2	8.3	7.0	—	.7

TEXAS

EXXON	16.0	15.2	14.3	16.3	+	.3
TEXACO	15.1	14.6	14.4	14.2	—	.9
GULF	10.4	9.7	9.4	9.9	—	.5
MOBIL	7.6	7.4	7.4	7.7	+	.1
SHAMROCK	5.2	5.9	6.0	5.9	+	.7

UTAH

CHEVRON	14.2	14.4	14.6	15.0	+	.8
AMOCO	13.2	14.0	13.3	13.8	+	.6
PHILLIPS	11.5	10.6	10.3	10.2	—	1.3
HUSKY	13.9	11.1	9.6	8.6	—	5.3
TEXACO	7.5	7.2	7.4	7.9	+	.4

(Continued)

VERMONT

MOBIL	16.9	16.9	16.6	16.5	— .4
TEXACO	15.1	14.2	13.4	13.5	— 1.6
GULF	11.6	10.3	9.7	9.7	— 1.9
EXXON	9.6	9.4	8.7	8.7	— .9
SHELL	10.0	9.2	8.4	8.4	— 1.6

VIRGINIA

EXXON	19.1	18.1	17.2	18.9	— .2
TEXACO	12.4	12.8	12.3	12.3	— .1
GULF	8.7	8.4	8.7	9.2	— .5
SHELL	8.0	7.7	6.9	6.8	— 1.2
AMOCO	7.3	6.8	6.4	6.5	— .8

WASHINGTON

SOCAL	18.8	17.9	14.7	15.8	— 3.0
ARCO	11.2	12.3	12.4	12.8	+ 1.6
TEXACO	11.9	13.9	11.6	11.2	— .7
SHELL	12.5	10.5	11.0	10.8	— 1.7
UNION	7.8	8.0	8.3	8.9	+ 1.1

WEST VIRGINIA

EXXON	21.9	20.9	19.6	20.1	— 1.9
ASHLAND	11.2	12.4	13.7	16.1	+ 4.9
GULF	11.5	10.0	10.4	9.9	— 1.6
TEXACO	7.5	8.0	8.8	8.2	+ .7
UNION	7.9	8.4	7.7	6.5	— .6

WISCONSIN

AMOCO	15.3	14.7	14.2	14.9	— .4
MOBIL	9.2	8.8	8.4	8.8	— .4
CLARK	—	—	5.6	6.4	+ 6.4
MURPHY	3.6	4.5	5.4	6.1	+ 2.5
TEXACO	6.0	6.2	5.5	5.3	— .7

WYOMING

AMOCO	13.8	13.3	12.8	12.7	— 1.1
TEXACO	12.1	12.1	12.7	11.7	— .4
CONOCO	12.9	12.1	11.7	11.2	— 1.7
LITTLE AMERICA	4.7	6.5	7.1	9.5	+ 4.8
HUSKY	7.0	7.0	7.2	6.5	— .5

Source: Lundberg Survey Data, *National Petroleum News,* various editions.

TABLE 10

THE TOP FIFTEEN INCREASES IN MARKET SHARES
ON THE STATE LEVEL
(1970-1973)

Rank	Share	State	Increase in Annual Average Market Shares (percentage points)
1	Tesoro	Alaska	20.1
2	Shell	Hawaii	9.0
3	Tosco	Arkansas	6.5
4	Seago Entr.	Mississippi	6.0
5	Little America	Wyoming	4.8
6	BP Oil	Maine	3.2
7	Shell	Arizona	3.0
8	Phillips	Nevada	2.9
9	Murphy	Wisconsin	2.5
10	ARCO	Oregon	2.4
11	Texaco	Oklahoma	2.3
12	Northwestern	Minnesota	2.1
13	ARCO	Delaware	2.0
14	Exxon	South Carolina	2.0
15	Amoco	South Dakota	2.0

Source: Table 9.

Table 10 summarizes Table 9. The data in Table 10 indicate which companies have experienced the largest increases in market shares in particular states. Four of the top five gainers, five of the top ten, and six of the top fifteen are nonbranded independent oil companies. The data do not suggest, in other words, any pronounced tendency for the major oil companies to increase their shares in particular states.

In only six states and the District of Columbia do the sales of a particular major brand exceed 20 percent of the market. Gasoline sales in Alaska are dominated by Socal, Texaco and Union. However, in the last three years Tesoro, an independent, has captured a significant portion of the market. Similarly, Hawaii is dominated by Socal and Shell. Exxon is strongly represented in West Virginia and the District of Columbia, while Sohio is dominant in Ohio and Amoco in North Dakota and South Dakota. Significantly, most of these states are either rural with small dispersed populations or are not contiguous with the lower 48 states. The District of Columbia is a concentrated urban area with competition from nearby sections of Maryland and Virginia. The remaining 44 states have even less concentrated markets for gasoline. In short, the charge that major companies dominate, or have increased their domination, in particular regions is not supported by the facts.

CHAPTER FOUR

Vertical Integration in The Petroleum Industry

The oil industry consists of four basic sectors—production, refining, marketing and transportation. Although most companies in the industry confine their operations to one of these sectors, the larger firms operate in two or more and all twenty of the largest companies operate in all four. Whenever a firm transmits from one sector to another a good or service that it could sell in the open market, it is said to be vertically integrated.[1]

Vertical integration in the oil industry has always been viewed with suspicion.[2] Now, as a result of widespread criticism of the industry, attention has once again focused on vertical integration and how it shapes the behavior of individual firms in the industry. Critics claim that vertically integrated firms are able to control the market to the detriment of both their nonintegrated rivals and American consumers. The result, they contend, has been a "substantial misallocation of society's scarce resources and . . . the imposition of substantial costs upon American consumers and taxpayers."[3]

Because of this charge, Congress is now considering various measures that would require vertical divestiture, that is, the separation of production, refining, transportation and marketing in

---

1. Adelman, Morris, "Integration and Antitrust Policy." *Harvard Law Review,* Volume 63, p. 27 (1949).

2. See, for example, *Hearings Before the Temporary National Economic Committee,* 76th Cong., 2nd & 3rd Sess., Parts 14-17A. Rostow, Eugene V. *A National Policy for the Oil Industry.* New Haven: Yale University Press, 1948.

3. Federal Trade Commission Staff. *Complaint Counsel's Prediscovery Statement, In the Matter of Exxon et al.,* Docket 8943, February 1974, p. 95.

the oil industry. On October 8, by a vote of 45-54, the Senate rejected an amendment to the Natural Gas Emergency Act that would have prohibited any major producer, refiner or transporter from owning or controlling operations at any other level of the industry.[4] Two weeks later the Senate defeated, by another close vote, an attempt to prohibit major producers from having any interest in refining, transportation or marketing.[5] Some senators voted against these amendments because they had not been formally considered and reported by the appropriate committee. For this reason, supporters of divestiture in Congress have announced that they will continue to hold hearings and will bring a bill to a vote later in the 94th Congress.

Several divestiture bills have been introduced in the Congress.[6] Like the amendments that were offered to the Natural Gas Emergency Act, some would prohibit all forms of vertical integration; other would only prohibit integration between certain sectors. Typically, the bills require the affected companies to prepare a divestiture plan and file it with the Federal Trade Commission. Once the Commission approves this plan, the companies must then sell off the forbidden assets within a specified period of time. In some bills, harsh criminal penalties would be imposed on the officers of companies not meeting the timetable set forth in the legislation.

Proponents of divestiture legislation believe that restructuring the petroleum industry is necessary for a number of reasons. First, they say that divestiture would increase competition at each and every stage of operation, and between stages, by creating many new companies competing with one another at arm's length. Second, supporters contend that this legislation would also decrease the potential for major company abuse of market power through joint ventures and exchange agreements. Third, divestiture would end major company ownership and control over crude and product pipelines and make it impossible for the major companies to squeeze

---

4. 121 *Cong. Rec.* S17864 (daily ed. Oct. 8, 1975).

5. 121 *Cong. Rec.* S18588 (daily ed. Oct. 22, 1975).

6. Perhaps the most important is S.2387, introduced by Senators Bayh, Abourezk, Philip Hart, Packwood and Tunney. Under S.2387, a major operator would be allowed to engage in only one sector of the industry. Or it would be allowed to split itself into smaller integrated units each falling under the size limits set by the bill. Only the largest producers, refiners, and marketers would be affected by S. 2387. However, all petroleum transportation and pipeline companies would be subject to divestiture. Significantly, major marketers would be permitted to retain or acquire refining interests although major refiners could not own marketing facilities. No reason has been given for this anomaly.

independent producers, refiners and marketers through control of these lines.

Finally, many industry critics believe that some kind of divestiture legislation is a necessary accompaniment to the decontrol of oil pricing and distribution. Without price and allocation controls to protect small and independent segments of the industry, these segments would very soon be driven out of business by the majors. Given their size, as well as their cooperative and interdependent behavior, the majors would, upon decontrol, have the power to administer prices to their own advantage.[7]

Many of these arguments appear in the Federal Trade Commission staff's antitrust suit against the eight largest oil companies. Although the FTC staff complaint does not specify the relief sought, the way the complaint is drawn and the way its arguments are advanced in supporting documents make it clear that vertical divestiture is seen as the appropriate remedy. The basic difference between Congressional efforts to achieve divestiture and the FTC staff's approach is in the forum used to reorganize the large oil companies. One is seeking a legislative solution; the other, divestiture through the judicial process.

How valid are these arguments against vertical integration? And what is likely to occur if either the courts or the Congress order divestiture? In this chapter, we will examine the arguments advanced in support of divestiture. In the following one we will discuss the probable impact of divestiture on the industry and the consuming public.

Two basic arguments have been advanced in support of the allegation that vertical integration is anticompetitive. First, vertical integration may allow market control in one segment of an industry to be extended to another.[8] For example, even though the refining industry may not be concentrated, the fact that relatively few companies control crude oil pipelines, it is argued, may give the integrated refiners unfair market power over independent refiners.[9]

---

7. See, for example, "Facts About Vertical Divestiture in the Oil Industry," issued jointly by Senators Hart (Mich.), Hart (Col.), Nelson and Abourezk, September 19, 1975.

8. Areeda, Phillip. *Antitrust Analysis,* second edition. Boston: Little, Brown and Co., 1974, pp. 675-6.

9. Rostow, Eugene V. *A National Policy for the Oil Industry.* pp. 57-66, and Rostow, Eugene V. and Sachs, Arthur S. "Entry into the Oil Refining Business: Vertical Integration Re-Examined." *Yale Law Review,* Volume 61, pp. 856 ff (1952).

This argument has been used in support of divestiture of the oil industry most recently in a report by the staff of the Senate Antitrust and Monopoly Subcommittee. In this report the subcommittee's staff states:

It is also important to recognize here that it is almost impossible to assess in isolation the degree of competition at any one level of the petroleum industry. The extent of cooperation or interdependence at any one level is affected by the community of interests that exists at the other levels. Regardless of the apparent structure at any one level, the dominance of the industry by the vertically integrated firms reduces competition at all levels to a sort of lowest common denominator. Each cooperative device at each level adds to the total effect. [10]

While correct in theory, this argument has little validity as it applies to the integrated oil companies. As we have already shown in Chapter 1, each segment of the oil industry is relatively unconcentrated. Therefore, it would appear unlikely that the "lowest common denominator" is low enough to permit significant anticompetitive potential to be transmitted from one segment of the industry to another.

However, even if vertically integrated oil companies could use their market power at one level to dominate another, this does not support the demands for divestiture. For one thing, it must be shown that the companies have in fact "combined their market influence for the purpose or with the effect of influencing price and restricting the opportunity of competitors to enter the field." [11] As we will show below, many of the often-cited examples of abuse arising from major company market power have actually been predictable responses to government price and allocation controls.

Even more to the point is the question of whether vertical divestiture is the appropriate remedy at all. Monopoly power, as Bork notes, is the result of horizontal market control. [12] If monopoly power in one segment is being extended to other segments of the industry because of vertical integration, the solution is not to attack vertical integration, but to attack the monopoly power at its source.

The second basic criticism of vertical integration in the oil industry

10. Senate Antitrust and Monopoly Subcommittee Staff, *Report*. Reprinted in 121 *Cong. Rec.* S16406 (daily ed., Sept. 22, 1975).

11. Rostow and Sachs, "Entry into the Oil Refinery Business. . .", p. 869.

12. Bork, Robert. "Vertical Integration and the Sherman Act: The Legal History of an Economic Misconception." *University of Chicago Law Review*. Volume 22, 1954, p. 201.

is that it enables price squeezes on independents, particularly independent refiners and marketers. Independents competing against vertically integrated firms face unfair competition, it is argued, because their competitors are also their suppliers. Thus, an integrated refiner can raise the price of the gasoline he sells to independent marketers and, in this way, either increase his share of the market or squeeze the profit margins of his independent competitors. Or, the integrated company can subsidize the market price for his product by means of higher prices for crude oil, again putting his independent competitors at an unfair disadvantage.

This argument against vertical integration suffers from several conceptual fallacies.[13] What remains when these fallacies are removed is the assertion that vertically integrated oil companies may engage in predatory pricing at certain levels of the industry using the profits derived from other levels. Whether vertical integration should be blamed for this behavior has been the subject of heated debate. Again, Bork argues that:

> Properly, "squeezes" should be regarded merely as price-cutting campaigns in the market affected. Otherwise the abuse becomes associated with the concept of vertical integration, although it does not spring from that form of organization at all.[14]

For all practical purposes, when reduced to these terms, the second argument against vertical integration is little different from the first. Vertical integration merely allows market control at one level of the industry to facilitate control at another. The relevant issue is, once again: Is there evidence of undue market power in a particular segment of the industry? And, if there is, will a vertical divestiture order dissolve this power?

Although, logically, the profit subsidization argument does not support divestiture, it has become the principal justification for a divestiture law. For this reason, in the remainder of this chapter we analyze this second argument at length. We focus on the work of two different groups who have devoted considerable effort to attacking vertical integration in the petroleum industry, the Federal Trade

---

13. For a convenient list of these fallacies, see *Ibid.*, pp. 198-200. See also Bork, Robert. "Contrasts in Antitrust Theory: I." *Columbia Law Review,* Volume 65, pp. 403-09 (1965); and Bork, Robert. "Vertical Integration and Competitive Processes." Weston and Peltzman, eds. *Public Policy Toward Mergers.* Pacific Palisades, Calif.: Goodyear Publishing Co., 1969.

14. Bork, "Vertical Integration and the Sherman Act," p. 165.

Commission staff[15] and Allvine and Patterson.[16]

Both the FTC staff and Allvine and Patterson begin their analyses of vertical integration by examining the relationship between crude production and refining. And both, in turn, rely on the work of DeChazeau and Kahn.[17] According to DeChazeau and Kahn, refiners with a sufficient supply of captive crude production are able to squeeze the profit margins of independent refiners and marketers. Their argument is as follows: A firm with crude production equal to its refinery output will be indifferent to the price of crude oil for any given product price because its total revenues and profits will remain the same. But because of the depletion allowance, a greater after-tax profit can be realized by minimizing downstream earnings while maximizing crude production earnings.

Beyond a certain level of self-sufficiency in crude oil, it is argued, integrated companies benefit from higher crude prices even if product prices remain unchanged. As a result, the majors have set artificially high crude prices and have earned an artificially low return on refining and marketing. This, in turn, has discouraged entry into the refining and marketing sector by nonintegrated firms. It has also made it difficult for existing nonintegrated refiners to survive.[18]

The FTC staff and Allvine and Patterson build on this foundation by analyzing the effect of oil import quotas on refiners.[19] According to both, the import quotas acted as a further barrier to entry in refining by restricting the supply of crude oil available to a potential entrant. The quotas also squeezed independent refiners' profit margins by raising the price of domestic crude. The FTC staff also argues that oil import quotas benefited integrated companies in other ways. Because import rights went only to existing firms, the majors were able to

---

15. FTC Staff, *Preliminary Report.* See also FTC Staff, *Prediscovery Statement.*

16. Allvine, Fred and Patterson, James. *Highway Robbery: An Analysis of the Gasoline Crisis.* Also statement of James Patterson, *Hearings on the Industrial Reorganization Act: the Energy Industry before the Subcommittee on Antitrust and Monopoly of the Senate Committee on the Judiciary,* 93d Cong., 2d Sess., pt. 8, 1974, pp. 6075-6103.

17. DeChazeau, Melvin G. and Kahn, Alfred E. *Integration and Competition in the Petroleum Industry.* New Haven: Yale University Press, 1959.

18. *Ibid.,* pp. 220-26.

19. Quotas were imposed in March 1959 by Presidential Proclamation 3279, 3 C.F.R. (1959-1963 Comp.) 11. Throughout their history they were extremely controversial. See Dam, Kenneth. "Implementation of Import Quotas: The Case of Oil." *Journal of Law and Economics,* Volume 14, pp. 1-73 (1971). They were lifted by Proclamation 4210, 3A C.F.R. (1973 Comp.) 60.

purchase oil at the lower world price, refine this oil, and then sell the products at the higher domestic price. In addition, the major oil companies were able to realize profits through trading for the import rights of inland domestic refiners. Often inland refiners were unable to refine imported oil and had no choice but to trade with the larger companies.[20] These advantages are why, according to Allvine and Patterson, the major oil companies were able to convince the government to impose quotas in the beginning. It also explains why these companies vigorously opposed the elimination of the quotas when this was proposed by the Cabinet Task Force in 1969.[21]

Both Allvine and Paterson and the FTC staff also argue that, because of recent changes in the world crude market, integrated companies are now shifting their interests to the marketing sector of the industry. To protect and enhance their position in marketing they are denying crude oil supplies to independent refiners who sell to independent marketers.[22] Finally, they suggest that the shortages of refined products that occurred prior to the Arab embargo were contrived by the major companies in order to drive the independents from the marketplace.[23]

Are these arguments valid? We begin with the DeChazeau and Kahn thesis, later adopted by Allvine and Patterson, that the depletion allowance favors integrated refiners over nonintegrated refiners. The short answer to this argument is that it is now irrelevant. Title V of the Tax Reduction Act of 1975 permanently repealed the depletion allowance for all integrated oil firms.[24] In fact, by retaining it for smaller, nonintegrated firms, the Act may actually encourage the divestiture of some crude oil production.

However, DeChazeau and Kahn and Allvine and Patterson wrote their books and the FTC staff brought its complaint against the majors before depletion was repealed. Was their argument correct prior to 1975? At issue is the degree of self-sufficiency in crude oil necessary for an integrated refiner to benefit from increases in the price of crude oil. The Commission staff claims that the threshold

---

20. FTC Staff, *Preliminary Report*, p. 15.
21. Allvine and Patterson, p. 29.
22. FTC Staff, *Prediscovery Statement*, pp. 88 and 93. Allvine and Patterson, p.30.
23. FTC Staff, *Prediscovery Statement*, p. 87. Allvine and Patterson, pp. 163-205.
24. P.L. 94-12. See McDonald, Stephen L. "Taxation System and Market Distortion." Kalter and Vogley, eds. *Energy Supply and Government Policy*, Syracuse, N.Y.: Cornell Univ. Press (forthcoming, Fall 1976) for a discussion of the Act and its effects on oil production.

level was 40 percent.[25] Richard Mancke of Tufts University has shown, however, that the figure was actually 93 percent.[26] Table 11 presents the Commission staff's own estimates of the domestic crude oil self-sufficiency of the 17 leading refiners in 1969. Only Getty, a firm not charged with antitrust violations by the FTC staff, meets the 93 percent test. In other words, if the integrated companies have deliberately concentrated their profits at the production level, as has been alleged, they have been operating in a way contrary to their own economic self-interest.[27]

Critics of vertical integration have also argued that oil import quotas contributed to the squeeze on independent refiners. Once again, the short answer is that the quotas have been abolished and the argument is now irrelevant.[28] But once again we consider at length the argument that the quota system hurt the independent refiners.

There is no question that the quotas restricted the supply of foreign crude available to U.S. refiners. This was their purpose. But it is not clear that the quotas squeezed the profit margins of independent refiners. In fact, the evidence points to just the opposite conclusion, that the quotas actually inflated the profit margins of small refiners. This is because the right to import oil was allocated by means of a sliding scale. The sliding scale worked like a graduated income tax in reverse: the smaller the refiner, the larger its allocation.

Table 12 compares quota allocations over the period 1959 to 1972. In 1959 a small refiner with a 10,000 bpd input received a quota of 1,140 barrels. By 1972 the quota had increased to 2,170. The right to import oil during the sixties was worth about $1.25 a barrel. Thus, a refiner with a 10,000 bpd input received a subsidy of approximately $520,125 in 1959 and $990,062 in 1972.

25. FTC Staff, *Preliminary Report*, p. 17.

26. Mancke, Richard. *The Failure of U.S. Energy Policy.* New York: Columbia University Press, 1974, pp. 173-4.

27. For a somewhat different analysis, with similar implications for the validity of this argument, see Erickson, Edward W., Millsaps, Stephen W. and Spann, Robert M. "Oil Supply and Tax Incentives," Okun and Perry, eds. *Brookings Papers on Economic Activity 1974, Vol. 2.* Washington, D.C.: The Brookings Institution, pp. 454-6.

28. The FTC Administrative Law Judge assigned to the FTC staff's case has recognized that depletion repeal and the abolition of the quotas have changed the case in fundamental ways and, for this reason, has recommended that the case be reconsidered. However, the Commision, on a 3-1 vote, has rejected this advice and directed that the prosecution continue. See *Oil and Gas Journal.* October 27, 1975, p. 50.

TABLE 11

THE FTC'S ESTIMATES OF THE DOMESTIC SELF-SUFFICIENCY OF 17 LEADING REFINERS IN 1969

Company	Self-Sufficiency (percent of runs to stills)
Standard (New Jersey)	87.4
Standard (Indiana)	50.5 (d)
Texaco	81.0 (e)
Shell	62.1
Standard (California)	68.8 (d)
Mobil	42.2 (a)
Gulf	87.6 (d,c)
Arco	64.9
Sun	46.7 (b)
Union	64.3 (d)
Standard (Ohio)	6.7 (d)
Phillips	51.8 (d)
Ashland*	12.6
Continental	64.0
Cities Service	49.9
Getty**	137.2 (c)
Marathon	88.1

(a) Other liquids included in refinery runs
(b) Crude production includes Canada
(c) Excludes crude processed for company's account
(d) Other liquids included in crude production
(e) Estimated

*Data cover the twelve months to September 30, 1969.
**Includes subsidiaries.

Source: *Preliminary Federal Trade Commission Staff Report on Its Investigation of the Petroleum Industry,* p. 20, based on estimates obtained from Kerr, Rice & Co., Engineers.

In fact, it has long been the conventional wisdom in the oil industry that during the 1960s some small refiners actually made most of their profits from sales of import tickets. What caused grief to these refiners was not vertical integration in the oil industry but the rise in the price of foreign oil relative to domestic oil after 1972. This depressed the price of import tickets, making it no longer so profitable for the integrated refiners to run foreign as domestic crude. In short, it is hard to support the claim that the quota system squeezed the profit margins of small, nonintegrated refiners. What is

TABLE 12

SLIDING SCALE ALLOCATIONS OF IMPORT QUOTAS
FOR VARIOUS PERIODS: 1959-1972

(PERCENTAGE OF REFINERY INPUTS)

Average bpd Input	Jul.-Dec. 1959	Jan.-Jun. 1964	Jan.-Dec. 1966	Jan.-Dec. 1970	Jan.-Dec. 1972
0-10,000	11.4	14.0	18.0	19.5	21.7
10,000-30,000	10.0	11.9	11.4	11.0	13.0
30,000-100,000	8.0	9.3	8.9	7.0	7.6
100,000 plus	6.0	5.5	5.3	3.0	3.8

*Sources: Shaffer, Edward. *The Oil Import Program of the United States.* New York: Praeger, 1968, p. 166; Dam, Kenneth. "Implementation of Import Quotas: The Case of Oil. *"Journal of Law and Economics,* Vol. 14, p. 21, (1971); National Petroleum Refiners Association, *Oil Import Digest,* Vol. 1. NPRA, 1975, p. A29. Data are for refiners located in Districts I-IV. For 1959, the figures are approximations because allocations were then made on the basis of nine categories of refiners.

more plausible is that the subsidy provided by the quotas kept some small, noneconomic refineries in business throughout the 1960's and early 1970's. This conclusion is supported by the testimony of the small refiners themselves.[29]

About 60 percent of the allocations made under the import quota system went to refiners with inputs greater than 70,000 bpd. Most of these refiners were integrated. Therefore, it is true, as the FTC argues, that most of the economic rents accruing from the quotas were received by large, integrated companies. But the FTC staff seems to imply that, because of their market power, the majors were able to realize some of the rents that would have accrued to the small refiners as well. Once again, this was not the case. After an initial period of adjustment when the quotas were first imposed, "All quota holders became assured of a relatively uniform premium in dollars and cents value for each barrel of oil exchanged."[30] In fact, for many years the government actually came to use the ticket price as a yardstick for determining whether to increase or reduce quota

---

29. See, for example, Cabinet Task Force on Oil Import Control. *The Oil Import Question.* Washington, D.C.: U.S. Government Printing Office, 1970, p. 261. See also statement by Edwin Dryer on behalf of Independent Refiners Association of America, *Hearings on the President's Energy Message and S.1570 Before the Senate Committee on Interior and Insular Affairs,* 93d Cong., 1st Sess., 1973, p. 541.

allocations. Stability of the ticket price paid to small refiners at or around $1.25 per barrel was, in effect, the U.S. import policy.

Given Allvine and Patterson's confusion about how the quota system operated, it is not surprising that the underlying motives of the companies have also been misunderstood. For example, although Allvine and Patterson assert that integrated companies were behind the push for import controls, the record is quite clear that the five largest international firms—Gulf, Mobil, Socal, Exxon and Texaco—all vigorously opposed the imposition of quota restrictions.[31] These companies had all made substantial investments in overseas crude production; it was contrary to their own economic self-interest to limit access by foreign crude to the U.S. market.

Some of these companies did oppose the lifting of import restrictions in 1969 when this was recommended by the Cabinet Task Force majority. But there were reasons for this stand other than a desire to harm independent refiners. Several major companies had now made sizable investments in offshore and Alaskan oil. Lifting import restrictions might reduce the value of these investments. Furthermore, support for the quota system insured good relations with small but politically powerful domestic producers. Perhaps most important, the Cabinet Task Force billed its proposals as a way of lowering domestic oil prices.[32] With this objective, few domestic oil companies—integrated or nonintegrated—were likely to support the Task Force's conclusions and recommendations.

The charges of widespread denial of supply to independent markets are difficult to assess because they are so unspecific. But one thing does bear mentioning. Of the seven independent marketers that Allvine and Patterson claim were cut off from supplies by integrated firms, none was directly supplied by an integrated company.[33] Instead, most of these companies had, in the past, bought product on

30. Material Relating to the Testimony of Professor Paul Homan, *Hearings on Govermental Intervention in the Market Mechanism Before the Subcommittee on Antitrust and Monopoly of the Senate Judiciary Committee,* 91st Cong., 1st Sess., pt. 1, 1969, p. 425.

31. See Mead, Walter. "Petroleum: An Unregulated Industry?" Kalter and Vogley, eds., *Energy Supply and Government Policy.* For a good discussion of the politics of the imposition of import controls, see Olson, David M. *The Government Relations Programs of the American Petroleum Institute and the IPAA: A Comparative Study.* Ph.D. dissertation, Univ. of California, 1962, Chapter 3.

32. See, for example, Wyant, William. "The Consumer Be Damned." *New Republic,* March 7, 1970, pp. 11-12; Francis, David. " 'Good Guys' Gunned Down." *Christian Science Monitor,* March 9, 1970.

33. Allvine and Patterson, pp. 171-180.

the spot market at distress prices.[34] This gave them a strong competitive position as long as there was excess refining capacity. During the early 1970's this surplus disappeared, primarily because of actions by federal, state and local governments. When shortages occurred, these firms were the first to feel them. Suppliers will always favor customers with whom they have long, established business relations.

A major reason why independent refiners were unable to obtain crude oil in 1973 was the Cost of Living Council's Special Rule Number 1.[35] Issued on March 6, 1973, this rule was designed to arrest the substantial rise in oil prices that occurred in early 1973 by restricting the large integrated companies to certain weighted average price increases over base period levels for all of their products. If the companies exceeded these increases they would trigger profit margin limitations that, in effect, would roll back their average prices.

Historically, many small refiners purchased crude oil from major oil companies by swapping their right to import their disproportionate share of low cost foreign oil for domestic crude produced by the larger oil companies. As long as the domestic price exceeded the foreign price, this exchange benefited both small and large refiners. Many of the integrated companies were willing to continue to swap crude with independent refiners in 1973, but at prices that reflected its replacement cost, i.e., the now higher prices for imported oil. But this would have used up much of the weighted average price increases allowed by Special Rule Number 1. Instead, a number of integrated companies chose to let the independent refiners fend for themselves. The integrated firms made very little return on the sale of crude oil to independent refiners; they were, essentially, middlemen. For this reason, when Special Rule Number 1 was promulgated, the majors had an incentive to abandon the small refiners they had previously supplied.

Parenthetically, Special Rule Number 1 encouraged similar behavior by the integrated companies toward independent distributors of propane. Some propane is produced in refineries. However, most is a by-product of the production of natural gas. Traditionally, the integrated companies have purchased propane from producers, combined it with propane produced in their own

---

34. For a discussion of these buying practices, see Reid, Marvin. "Caught in a Price Squeeze: What's the Future of the Private Brander?" *National Petroleum News,* January 1975, p. 55.

35. 38 F.R. 6283.

refineries, and have then sold it to distributors who, in turn, sell it to consumers. In 1973, the price of propane rose sharply, largely because of growing shortages of natural gas. (Propane is a close substitute for natural gas in many uses.) Here, too, the integrated oil companies were actually penalized by Special Rule Number 1 if they continued in their traditional role as middlemen supplying independent distributors of propane. Some of the companies ceased acting as middlemen and, as a result, traditional consumers of propane, such as farmers and low-income households, were faced with shortages and disruption in their normal source of supply.[36]

The majors received the blame. The real culprit, however, was the Cost of Living Council. Because of Special Rule Number 1, many independent refiners and propane consumers became strong advocates of the mandatory allocation of oil.

Allvine and Patterson also discuss how in 1972 and 1973 price controls on No. 2 fuel oil created potential home heating oil shortages in the nation.[37] They argue that the integrated companies deliberately refrained from petitioning the Price Commission for an increase in No. 2 fuel oil prices in order to insure a shortage and thus put a squeeze on independents. The truth, once again, is quite different. A history of oil price controls prepared by a former Cost of Living Council staff member reports that:

In the last quarter [of 1972], industry pressure increased steadily on the Price Commission to be receptive should refiners seek authorization to raise product prices, especially for home heating oil. . .The Price Commission, however, was not swayed and assured refiners that if formal application (prenotification) was made for increases, even if they were cost-justified, the increases would not be allowed without first holding public hearings on the whole question of oil pricing. This was a proceeding that promised to be lengthy and of decidedly negative public relations value to the companies. The Price Commission was not without support in its stand. New England Congressmen, worried about the potential shortage of heating oil, were demanding tight controls on home heating oil prices and had extracted a promise from the Administration that hearings would indeed be held before heating oil prices

---

36. See Johnson, William A. "The Impact of Price Controls on the Oil Industry." Eppen, Gary, ed. *Energy: The Policy Issues.* Chicago: University of Chicago Press, 1975. See also Langdon, Jr., James C. "FEA Price Controls for Crude Oil and Refined Petroleum Products." *26th Oil & Gas Inst.,* Matthew Bender, 1975.

37. Allvine and Patterson, pp. 165-204.

were allowed to go up.[38]

In short, the facts simply do not support the arguments made by Allvine and Patterson and the FTC staff against vertical integration of the oil industry and in favor of divestiture. In general, their arguments are either irrelevant, out of date, or wrong.

---

38. Department of the Treasury, Office of Economic Stabilization, *Historical Working Papers on the Economic Stabilization Program, History of Petroleum Price Controls.* Washington, D.C.: U.S. Government Printing Office, 1974, pp. 1236-7. For earlier examples of political pressures brought to bear to keep heating oil prices low see "Watchdogs Bark at Oil Prices." *Business Week.* August 31, 1968; "Humble Says Fuel Oil Prices Not Predatory." *Oil and Gas Journal.* October 26, 1970.

CHAPTER FIVE

The Effects of Vertical Divestiture

A corporation may integrate vertically for many reasons.[1] For example, McLean and Haigh have suggested that, because profits at the different levels of the industry are not closely related, vertical integration is one way of diversifying investment and stabilizing earnings. They also note that vertical integration reduces the risks associated with investment in highly capital-intensive facilities like refineries by assuring inputs of crude oil and markets for refined products. Finally, economies of management may be realized if operations in the different sectors of the industry can be coordinated.[2]

Mitchell has added still another reason that is especially relevant today: uncertainty created by federal price controls.[3] One way of avoiding the effects of price controls, Mitchell argues, is through vertical integration. Several firms, including Dow Chemical, General Motors, and Regis Paper, have been integrating into crude oil and natural gas production apparently to avoid shortages resulting from existing federal regulations.

---

1. See Kessler, Friedrich and Stern, Richard. "Competition, Contract and Vertical Integration." *Yale Law Journal,* Volume 69, (1959), pp. 2-14, for an extensive list of these reasons.

2. McLean, John and Haigh, Robert. *The Growth of the Integrated Oil Companies.* Cambridge: Harvard University Press, 1954.

3. Statement of Edward Mitchell, *Hearings on the Industrial Reorganization Act: the Energy Industry,* pp. 6065-6066.

Let us suppose that the oil companies are ordered to divest themselves of their operations in more than one sector of the industry. What might be the results of such an order? First, divestiture may well increase U.S. independence on foreign oil and therefore U.S. vulnerability to another oil embargo. The United States is now and will likely continue to be for at least the next decade dependent on foreign oil. Neither the North Slope, the Outer Continental Shelf nor Project Independence is going to make the U.S. self-sufficient in petroleum, particularly in the face of a prolonged economic recovery. Given this, do we or do we not prefer the large international oil companies to continue their special relationship with the United States? During the 1973 embargo, the international companies followed a policy of "equal suffering." In effect, they required nations deemed "friendly" by the Arabs, such as France, Spain and the United Kingdom, to share some of the shortages intended primarily for the United States.[4] A major reason for this (although not the only reason) was the substantial downstream investment by the international oil companies in the United States. Integration gave the majors an incentive to supply the United States with more crude oil than the Arab nations would have allowed had their embargo been fully effective.[5]

It is at least worth pondering whether the multinational companies would continue in their protective role toward U.S. downstream activities in another embargo if forced to choose between production or downstream operations. Indeed, if faced with divestiture, what might the majors give up? Those with significant foreign operations may give up their domestic operations.

In fact, with divestiture a common interest between the majors and OPEC might be forged in which the companies decide that their future interest and perhaps even their future survival depend upon

---

4. U.S. Senate, Committee on Foreign Relations, *Multinational Oil Corporations and U.S. Foreign Policy,* 93rd Cong., 2nd Sess., Jan. 1975. See also Stobaugh, Robert B. "The Oil Companies in the Crisis." *Daedalus,* Fall 1975, pp. 192-198. Also Commission of the European Communities. *Report by the Commission on the Behavior of the Oil Companies in the Community During the Period from October 1973 to March 1974.* Brussels, December 1975.

5. The principal means by which the companies shared the shortage during the embargo involved swapping non-Arab oil destined for "friendly" or "neutral" nations for Arab oil normally destined for the United States. At the onset of the embargo, the Treasury Department estimated that a fully effective embargo would have denied the United States about 2.8 million barrels per day. In fact, at worst, the shortage reached only half this amount.

cooperation with producers outside the United States. Some majors may decide to become marketing outlets for OPEC oil in the United States and Europe. Recent moves by OPEC members to reduce equity participation in production by the major companies have had the effect of divorcing company from producing country interests. Divestiture in the United States may actually help effect a reconciliation. The combined effect of the international oil companies and the OPEC cartel would be formidable.

At the production level, we may witness even more joint ventures and greater cooperation between newly divorced producers of crude oil. With their equity base and cash flow greatly diminished, even previously small investments may, because of the risk, become too costly to bear alone. Growth in the size of companies engaged in exploration and greater concentration in new production would help to offset the greater risks inherent in exploration and development than exist in other segments of the industry.

At the transportation level, divestiture would require new "arm's length" relationships between producers and pipelines. This would almost certainly impose higher costs on consumers. Pipelines are expensive and economic only when run at or near capacity. Under divestiture, pipeline companies may find themselves operating at less than full capacity. And even if the companies were able to execute contracts with producers and refiners that insure operation at full capacity, their "transaction costs" would almost certainly be higher than before the divestiture occurred. The Interstate Commerce Commission would have to raise pipeline rates or face future shortages in pipeline capacity. Again, consumers would have to pay more for their oil.

Greater concentration as a result of divorcement seems less likely in refining than in other segments of the industry. Most refineries are built to optimum capacity and technology for the crude they use and the market they serve. The problem in the refining sector in recent years has been inadequate profitability. Many refineries are now actually operating at a loss, in part, because of the government's price controls.[6] Divorcement will require higher rates of return and, in

---

6. See the comments of several major oil company executives to this effect in "How Controls Transformed Marketing—Then and Now." *National Petroleum News,* October 1975, pp. 36-37.

general, higher refined product prices.[7]

Moreover, it is unlikely that divestiture would bring with it a large increase in U.S. refining capacity. Divestiture may, in fact, encourage expatriation of U.S. refining capacity and, in this way, undermine the beneficial effects of the 1973 changes in the oil import program.[8] In other words, the United States may be damned by divestiture one way or the other. If foreign holdings are included in a divestiture order, some companies may divest their domestic operations; if they are not, they would have an incentive to shift their new investments, particularly in production and refining, to foreign countries in order to circumvent a divestiture ruling.

Marketing is a highly competitive sector of the industry. Its competitiveness may also be affected adversely by divestiture. Over the past decade independent marketers have had an increasing share of the market at the expense of major branded outlets. One reason for this has been an almost chronic excess refining capacity which has, in turn, created spot markets for gasoline and other refined products. With the exception of 1973-74, excess capacity has been the prevailing state in the industry. Under divestiture, this excess capacity would probably disappear.

Marketing is now a relatively depressed segment of the industry. It now seems clear that the industry will have to move toward higher volume sales. Divestiture would probably give further impetus to concentration in marketing. It may well be the catalyst that speeds the creation of a relatively few high-volume outlets and the demise of many small jobbers and marketers. Many of the services now provided to dealers and small jobbers by the major oil companies such as dealer training, business improvement loans, and management consulting, would probably be taken over by the newly created large-volume marketers.[9]

Existing high-volume independent jobbers would be in the best

---

7. Others have noted that a refining industry forced into arm's length bargaining for raw materials and pipeline usage would require greater operating margins to cover its greater risks. Reduced assurance of continuous flows into and out of a refinery would also raise capital costs. See DeChazeau and Kahn, p. 356.

8. By imposing higher fees on refined products than on crude oil, the April 1973 changes sought to reverse the trend toward building refineries outside the United States. See statement by William E. Simon, then Deputy Secretary of the Treasury, on the Oil Import Program, April 18, 1973, reprinted in *Hearings on the Energy Conservation and Conversion Act of 1975 Before the Senate Committee on Finance*, 94th Cong., 1st Sess., pt. 1, pp. 309-312.

9. DeChazeau and Kahn, p. 517.

position to buy up major oil company marketing operations. Some divestiture bills would actually permit these jobbers to enlarge and integrate backward into refining. With this bonus, the marketing segment of the industry may quickly become dominated by giant semi-integrated companies. Once the major company umbrella is removed from the smaller branded and nonbranded marketers who are affiliated with the majors, these marketers may find themselves either absorbed into new marketing conglomerates or reduced to a position in which they cannot compete profitably.

Branded jobbers and major oil compnay lessees, especially, are likely to be hardest hit by divestiture. They would lose the benefits of credit cards, advertising and other services provided by major oil company suppliers. Most importantly, they would lose an assured source of supply. Supplier relationships built up over many years would be destroyed.

Underlying the argument throughout this section is a prospect ignored by critics of vertical integration of the oil industry: Without the major integrated companies there could be rather significant horizontal mergers and greater concentration in all four segments of the industry. No one knows how much concentration would occur after vertical divestiture. However, it is widely recognized that the majors are now restrained from excessive growth because they fear existing antitrust laws. For this reason, integration has in a very real sense been an alternative to concentration and, in this way, has actually provided protection for many small and independent companies in the industry.

Some critics of divestiture argue that it would disrupt capital markets and almost certainly depress the prices of oil company securities, in this way reducing the assets of millions of industry shareholders.[10] On the other hand, supporters argue that the larger integrated oil companies would not have to sell off shares if ordered to divest. Rather, the companies could simply divide themselves vertically or horizontally in order to fall within the restrictions set by law. For example, under S.2387 a shareholder in Exxon could either become a shareholder in four separate firms producing, transporting, refining and selling oil, or a shareholder in a pipeline company and

---

10. See, for example, Statement of Raymond Gary, Managing Director of Morgan Stanley & Co., before the Senate Antitrust and Monopoly Subcommittee, January 27, 1976 (mimeo). See, also, First National City Bank, Petroleum Department, *Energy Memo*, Volume 12, January, 1976.

several small integrated companies, each falling within the size limits set by the law. It probably would not be that simple, but whether the impact of divestiture on shareholders would be as serious as some allege is anyone's guess. Divestiture would certainly create confusion in the oil industry and divert industry talents to reorganization at a time when they might better be applied to efforts to achieve U.S. energy self-sufficiency. It would also result in higher prices to consumers. This would occur in several ways.

First, managerial and other administrative services would necessarily be duplicated. There would have to be additional staff and facilities at all levels of the industry and, as a result, higher prices for consumers to cover these additional costs.

Second, the industry would have to increase its working stocks and storage facilities at the refinery level.[11] An integrated oil company's refinery is usually designed to run a certain blend of crude oil from several sources; it typically does not have sufficient blending capacity at its refineries. Instead, the integrated company mixes the crude oil from its captive wells or other sources in a pipeline system which it partially owns. The integrated company can do without substantial storage and blending facilities at its refinery because it has control of its crude oil at all stages of production and transportation. As a rule, it can schedule deliveries to meet its own refinery's needs.

However, if it did not have this ability—as it would not after divestiture—a refinery company, to err on the safe side, would have to have substantially greater working stocks of the various types of crude oil that it uses. It would also have to have additional blending tanks within its perimeters.

One way to get around this problem would be for the refinery to adjust its operations from time to time to accommodate different types of crude oil. In some instances, this would be impossible or impractical. For example, a particular refinery may be unable to use high sulfur crude oil because it would corrode its equipment. At present, the refinery may avoid this problem by blending its high and low sulfur crudes in its pipeline system, or the refinery might be able to make adjustments to accommodate different qualities of crude oils. These adjustments would, however, involve some down time which, in turn, would mean unutilized refinery capacity, lower production of refined products, and higher costs to consumers.

---

11. See Statement by Walter Peirson, President of Amoco Oil, *Hearings on the Petroleum Industry Before the Subcommittee on Antitrust and Monopoly of the Senate Judiciary Committee,* 94th Cong., 1st Sess., pt. 1, 1975, p. 368.

The same is true at the wellhead. One reason why the integrated companies often do not have sufficient storage facilities at their wells is that, in effect, their pipelines serve this function for them. As a result of divestiture, newly independent producers may have to increase their storage capability, and their working stocks, to protect against surges in demand and changes in pipeline availablilty.

Higher prices would also result from the substitution of market transactions for internal transfers between departments. As Williamson has observed:

> In more numerous respects than are commonly appreciated the substitution of internal organization for market exchange is attractive less on account of technological economies associated with production than because of what may be referred to broadly as "transactional failures" in the operations of markets for intermediate goods.[12]

For example, when long-term investments are associated with the performance of a contract, as is the case when a refinery is built to operate on a specific type of crude oil, the investment is highly vulnerable to contract performance problems. This vulnerability, and therefore the risk associated with the investment, is reduced by substituting the ownership of crude supplies for long-term crude supply contracts.[13]

In short, divestiture will not be cost-free to society. It is likely to discourage investment in the industry, require duplication of facilities, and result in higher prices to American consumers. Will the benefits of divestiture justify its costs? We are inclined to doubt it. In its deliberations, the Congress should make some effort to tally these costs before acting to break up the vertically integrated companies on the assumption that the public would be certain to benefit.

While it is deliberating divestiture, Congress might also want to consider other fundamental issues such as: Why is special antitrust legislation for the oil industry necessary? What kind of precedent is being set by enacting legislation aimed at only a few companies? Are existing antitrust laws inadequate to cope with the problems of competition in the oil industry?

The Sherman Act is the basic antitrust statute. It prohibits any contract, combination or conspiracy in restraint of trade and makes it

---

12. Williamson, Oliver. "The Vertical Integration of Production: Market Failure Considerations." *American Economic Review,* Volume 61, May 1971, p. 112.

13. The example is Mitchell's. See his Statement before the Senate Antitrust and Monopoly Subcommittee, January 22, 1976 (mimeo) for a further development of this argument.

illegal for any person to monopolize any part of such commerce. In judging whether a contract or combination is illegal, courts will apply the "Rule of Reason" and attempt to balance any anticompetitive effects against the benefits likely to result from such a contract. However, five types of business restraints are declared unreasonable *per se*. They are: (1) price fixing among competitors; (2) agreements to limit production; (3) agreements to divide markets; (4) resale price maintenance agreements; and (5) group boycotts or concerted refusals to deal with other companies.

Section 5 of the Federal Trade Commission Act makes unlawful "unfair methods of competition and unfair or deceptive acts or practices." The Commission has wide discretion in declaring trade practices to be unfair and ordinarily the courts will not question the Commission's judgment.[14] Section 5 also covers conduct which does not yet violate the Sherman Act but may be expected to do so if allowed to continue.[15] The FTC staff has brought its complaint against the eight largest oil companies under Section 5.

In contrast to the general provisions of the Sherman and Federal Trade Commission Acts, the Clayton Act is narrowly drawn. Section 2, as amended by the Robinson-Patman Act, prohibits price and service discrimination. This section provides protection to small companies like independent gasoline marketers who purchase their supplies wholesale from large companies and, at the same time, compete with the supplier at the retail level. Section 3 covers exclusive arrangements and tying clauses. Finally, Section 7 prevents a corporation from obtaining the assets of any other corporation "where in any line of commerce in any section of the country, the effect of such acquisition may be substantially to lessen competition, or tend to create a monopoly."[16]

Why then, with this substantial body of statutory and case law and adequate remedies available at law and equity, is special divestiture legislation for the oil industry necessary at this time? Perhaps it is because, as some critics claim, the laws are never vigorously enforced. Yet, between 1963 and 1973 the Justice Department initiated 224 separate investigations into industry practices and brought 40 formal complaints.[17] And indeed, many of the landmark

14. *Federal Trade Commission v. Brown Shoe Co.,* 384 U.S. 316 (1966). Because of the wide latitude afforded to the Commission under this section antitrust lawyers often refer to it as the "loophole section."

15. *Federal Trade Commission v. Cement Institute,* 333 U.S. 683 (1948).

16. For a more complete discussion of the antitrust laws, see Oppenhein, S. and Weston, G. *Federal Antitrust Laws: Cases and Comments*. St. Paul, Minn.: West Publishing Co., 1968. See, also, Van Cise, Jerold G. *The Federal Antitrust Laws,* 3d Ed. Washington, D.C.: American Enterprise Institute, 1975.

cases in antitrust law are oil industry cases.[18]

Another justification given for divestiture legislation is that, when the Justice Department or the Federal Trade Commission do bring a case, they inevitably lose because they are understaffed and poorly funded. Divestiture legislation, however, is an extreme remedy for this problem. Instead it would seem more appropriate to budget greater funds for federal antitrust activities.[19]

A third justification given by proponents of divestiture is that it takes too long to secure divestiture through the judicial process. For example, the FTC staff estimates that it will require three more years of investigation, together with an analysis of several million documents and the depositions of 500 to 700 industry officials before its case is ready for trial.[20] Divestiture legislation would circumvent an enormous amount of red tape. However, it would clear away this red tape by declaring the industry guilty of antitrust violations by legislative fiat rather than by the decision of the courts.

Circumventing the judicial process through legislation has its advantages; however, it also has its pitfalls. Justice Story has written of these pitfalls in his discussion of bills of atainder:

> In such cases, the legislature assumes judicial magistracy, pronouncing upon the guilt of the party without any of the common forms and guards of trial, and satisfying itself with proofs, when such proofs are within its reach, whether they are conformable to the rules of evidence, or not. In short, in all such cases, the legislature exercises the highest power of sovereignty, *and what may be properly deemed an irresponsible despotic discretion, being governed solely by what it deems political necessity or expediency, and too often under the influence of unreasonable fears, or unfounded suspicions.*[21]

---

17. Statement of Deputy Assistant Attorney General Bruce Wilson, *Hearings on Market Performance and Competition in the Petroleum Industry Before the Special Subcommittee on Integrated Oil Operations of the Senate Interior Committee,* 93d Cong., 1st Sess., 1973, p. 417.

18. For example, *Standard Oil Co. v. United States,* 221 U.S. 1 (1911); *United States v. Socony-Vacuum Oil Co.,* 310 U.S. 150 (1940); *Standard Oil Co. of California v. United States,* 337 U.S. 293 (1949).

19. This is, in fact, what is happening. The Federal Trade Commission has requested $6 million for fiscal year 1977 for its case against the major oil companies. See *Wall Street Journal,* Jan. 22, 1976.

20. Federal Trade Commission, *Certification to Commission of Recommendation of Administrative Law Judge that Commission Consider Withdrawal of Complaint In the Matter of Exxon, et al.,* Docket No. 8934 (Oct. 1975), p. 4.

21. Story, Joseph. *Commentaries on the Constitution of the United States,* Vol. 3. New York: DaCapo, 1970, 1833, Section 1338.

Whether a divestiture bill could survive a challenge on grounds that it is a bill of attainder is anyone's guess; the Supreme Court's latest opinion on the issue leaves the matter in some doubt.[22]

However, one thing is certain: a divestiture law will be challenged in the courts. And, whatever the outcome, the litigation would drag on for years.[23] In the meantime, few investors are likely to show much interest in the oil industry. This would occur at precisely the time when it is in the national interest to increase investment in the industry in order to advance the goal of U.S. energy self-sufficiency.

22. *United States v. Brown,* 381 U.S. 437 (1965).

23. One estimate is ten years before the issues raised by divestiture would be resolved in the courts. See Statement of Peter A. Bator before the Senate Subcommittee on Antitrust and Monopoly, January 27, 1976 (mimeo) p. 4.

CHAPTER SIX

Horizontal Integration in The "Energy Industry"

Horizontal integration in the energy industry is also under attack. Since the mid-1950s many of the larger oil companies have diversified into alternative energy sources, such as coal and uranium. It is claimed by some critics of the industry that this diversification is anticompetitive. Horizontal integration, it is thought, reduces the number of competing companies in the "energy industry." For this reason, legislation must be passed to preserve competition by preventing this practice.

For example, some critics argue that the oil industry, by aggressive promotion of the use of oil and natural gas as a boiler fuel, helped to undermine coal's last major market, the electric utilities, during the 1960s. Because of the oil companies' actions, it is alleged, the coal industry was depressed, thus permitting the coal companies to be bought up at bargain prices.

It is also argued that the participation of petroleum companies in the development of substitute fuels, such as coal and oil shale, involves an inherent conflict of interest. Oil companies controlling coal and oil shale ventures may not prove especially diligent in pushing new advances in technology if these advances undermine the future profitability of oil. Those oil companies with substantial interests in oil production will have an incentive to try to prevent the development of low-cost alternative sources of energy.[1]

---

1. One often cited example was Standard Oil's entry into synthetic fuels in the 1920's, allegedly to assure that the development of synthetics was kept in "friendly hands." DeChazeau and Kahn, p. 286. See also Stocking, George W. and Watkins, Myron W. *Cartels in Action.* New York: Twentieth Century Fund, 1946, p. 92.

A recent study for the Brookings Institution asserts that oil companies will be reluctant to develop oil shale for this reason.[2] However, this argument suffers from the same fallacy as the argument by Allvine and Patterson, discussed in Chapter Four. For an integrated oil company to benefit by limiting development of low cost synthetic fuels, it must have a substantial interest in production relative to such downstream activities as refining and marketing. In fact, all but one of the major integrated oil companies are net purchasers of crude oil.[3] As a group they must purchase crude oil from independent producers in order to keep their refineries operating at reasonably full capacity. Or, they must purchase crude oil from abroad, most likely from countries where they now have a limited equity position and earn little if any profit because of recent actions by the OPEC countries.

It is because most integrated oil companies are net purchasers of crude oil that several of these companies actually urged the government to put a lid on domestic crude oil prices in 1973 when domestic prices began to rise in response to price increases by the OPEC countries.[4] In short, it is not at all clear that the integrated oil companies lack incentive to develop low cost alternatives to conventional crude oil, if they exist. This incentive actually results from their substantial investment in refining operations.

In October 1975 an amendment to the Emergency Natural Gas Act requiring horizontal divestiture was defeated in the Senate by a vote of 39 to 53. As with the amendment requiring vertical divestiture, several Senators voted in the opposition, not because they opposed horizontal divestiture, but because the amendment was introduced without benefit of hearings or public comment. For this reason, S.489, the Interfuel Competition Act of 1975, is now under consideration in committee. In general, this bill would prevent any company involved in the production or refining of petroleum or natural gas from owning any assets in other energy industries. S.489 defines six basic energy activities other than oil and gas: coal, oil shale, uranium, nuclear reactors, geothermal energy, and solar energy. It would be unlawful for any company engaged in the production and refining of petroleum and/or natural gas to acquire any interest in these other energy activities. It would also be illegal to own or control any of these activities three years after the bill's

---

2. Davidson, Paul, Falk, Laurence H. and Lee, Hoesung. "Oil: Its Time Allocation and Project Independence," *Brookings Papers on Economic Activity, Volume 2.* Washington, D.C.: The Brookings Institution, 1974, p. 429.

3. See Table 11.

4. Personal experience of senior author. These companies included two of the eight largest majors, both of them relatively crude short.

enactment. In other words, oil and gas companies would have three years to divest themselves of existing horizontally integrated operations.

Unlike S.2387, which calls for vertical divestiture, S.489 does not apply only to the largest companies in the oil industry. Small independent producers and refiners could not be horizontally integrated under this bill.[5] It should also be noted that S.489, like S.2387, gives preferential treatment to marketers of oil and natural gas. This segment of the petroleum industry could, in theory at least, remain horizontally integrated. In addition, S.489 would apparently allow any petroleum or natural gas transporter to integrate horizontally into non-oil and gas activities. No reason has been given for these anomalies.

To assess the benefits and costs of horizontal divestiture, it is first necessary to understand what is meant by "horizontal integration." As it has been used in the study of industrial organization, "horizontal integration" has meant expansion within a particular stage of production in a particular industry. For example, the acquisition by a refiner of new refineries would constitute horizontal integration in the traditional sense of the word. In the current debate, the term "horizontal integration" is now being used more broadly to describe the diversification of petroleum companies outside of the petroleum industry but within the "energy industry." Critics argue that diversification into alternative fuels limits competition in the energy industry as a whole.

Implicit in this argument are several doubtful assumptions. First, it is assumed that there is an energy industry. This, in turn, assumes that the consumer is able to switch easily from one energy source to another. If so, the petroleum, coal, nuclear, and other energy industries would actually be parts of a single "energy industry." If alternative energy sources were readily available and substitutable, they would all be competing elements of a larger industry. Given this concept of the energy industry, it makes little difference whether a company expands operations within a particular energy subindustry or across energy subindustries. In either case, the level of competition in the energy industry as a whole is reduced because any company expansion or acquisition increases energy industry concentration.[6]

---

5. A number of the smaller oil companies are involved in the development of alternative fuels. An example is TOSCO, which is working in oil shale. Another is Champlin (Union Pacific), which has investments in coal.

6. The argument is developed by the FTC staff in Federal Trade Commission, *Concentration Levels and Trends in the Energy Sector of the U.S. Economy, Staff Report to the Federal Trade Commission.* Washington, D.C.: Government Printing Office, March 1974.

The issue of horizontal integration and divestiture is not so simple as this reasoning might imply. In many uses, alternative energy forms are not substitutable. For instance, one cannot burn coal in an automobile. Nor can one use uranium in an airplane, at least with today's technology. To the extent that alternative energy sources do not compete with one another in the same markets, the concept of an "energy industry" is inappropriate and misleading.

To say that alternative energy sources are not readily available and substitutable in all markets does not, of course, completely dismiss the argument against horizontal integration. Under certain circumstances and in certain markets the expansion of one company, whether by development of a new company or acquisition of an existing company, would increase concentration and reduce competition. For example, an electric power plant capable of using natural gas, coal, or fuel oil might be put at a considerable competitive disadvantage if formerly independent suppliers of these fuels were to merge. If there were no other competing sellers of these fuels, the electric power plant would face a monopoly and would not be able to use as a bargaining lever the fact that it might turn to alternative sources of supply.[7] And, even if there were additional suppliers for one or more alternative fuel inputs, collusion by the now smaller number of competitors would be easier. Thus, while the cost of horizontal integration in terms of potential competition foregone may not be so great as some believe, this cost cannot be dismissed either.

The obvious question at this point is: How significant has the trend been toward concentration in the "energy industry" as opposed to concentration in its components—the petroleum, gas, coal, and nuclear power industries? The FTC staff has concluded in its study of interfuel concentration that horizontal concentration has not been significant.

In the national energy market made up of all four fuels combined (oil, gas coal, and nuclear), concentration. . .is lower than the average concentration in the four separate fuels. . .
The reason that energy concentration is lower than the concentration in the separate fuels is that, although the large petroleum companies are both large crude oil producers and large natural gas producers, at the current time most of the large coal and uranium companies are not owned by petroleum com-

---

7. The same result would occur if the utility were prohibited by law from using all but one of these fuels. Section 101 of the Energy Policy and Conservation Act gives the FEA Administrator the authority to dictate to utilities what fuels they may or may not burn. How the exercise of this authority will affect the bargaining leverage of the utilities remains to be seen.

panies. Concentration is also low compared to many other industries.[8]

The FTC staff goes on to state that reserves of the four fuels have recently become more concentrated than production. For this reason, downstream operations in the separate fuel industries and in the energy industry as a whole may become more concentrated in the future. Thus, the Federal Trade Commission staff report recommends that both interfuel and intrafuel mergers should be given close scrutiny. The report does not recommend, however, horizontal divestiture or other more extreme remedies.[9]

Some supporters of horizontal divestiture have failed to recognize that important benefits are derived from horizontal integration. Perhaps most important, economies can be realized by bringing overlapping technology and operations under one management system. For example, exploration for petroleum, coal, and uranium have much in common. Oil and gas are often by-products of drilling, while research and development in coal gasification and liquefaction may be advanced by on-going research and development in the oil and gas industry. Successful commercial development of oil shale would seem to suggest a need for techniques and abilities that span both the petroleum and coal industries.[10]

In view of these economies, it is not surprising that Edwin Mansfield would find a sample of executives in the coal, petroleum, and electrical equipment industries feeling without exception that the acquisition of coal firms by petroleum companies would stimulate development of coal gasification, liquefaction, and other innovations in energy production. Oil companies would, they thought, devote expertise and capital that would not otherwise be available for development of synthetic fuels.[11] This belief is borne out by the fact that, between January 1964 and June 1974, 49 of 52 patents received by coal companies for coal conversion were received by the relatively few coal companies owned by oil companies.[12]

---

8. FTC Staff, *Concentration Levels and Trends,* pp. 147-148 (parentheses supplied).

9. This view is shared by more than just the authors of that study. See Statement of Owen Johnson, FTC staff member, before the Senate Antitrust and Monopoly Subcommittee, October 21, 1975 (mimeo); and Statement of F.M. Scherer, FTC staff member, before the Joint Economic Committee, November 19, 1975 (mimeo).

10. See Statement of C. Howard Hardesty before the Subcommittee on Energy of the Joint Economic Committee, November 19, 1975 (mimeo), pp. 3-8.

11. Edwin Mansfield, "Firm Size and Technological Change in the Petroleum and Bituminous Coal Industries," in Thomas D. Duchesneau, *Competition in the Energy Industry, p. 342.*

12. Canes, Michael. *Oil Firm Acquisition of Coal and Uranium Assets.* Unpublished paper, American Petroleum Institute, January, 1975.

Another advantage of horizontal integration is flexibility. Diversified companies are better able to mobilize the capital for expansion of needed energy activities. Horizontal diversification allows a company in a declining industry to expand in a growing industry. Simply put, it enables the optimal use of scarce resources. Claude Brinegar, now Senior Vice President of Union Oil Company, has put the issue succinctly: "If you legislatively build a fence around our future activities, you are sentencing us to a slow death."[13] One reason why many oil companies are showing increasing interest in synthetic oil and gas is that onshore U.S. oil production is declining. Synthetics made from coal and oil shale are seen as major future sources of raw material by the oil industry. By contrast, reliance on a finite source of supply would condemn the industry to a finite future.

It is now the stated policy of the government to develop the United States' extensive coal and shale oil reserves as fast as possible, within constraints imposed by the need to protect the environment. It is also national policy to reduce U.S. dependence on imported oil. Presumably, there should be no objection to the oil companies' investing their resources in these alternative energy industries. This is what the government wants; it is also what the current relative profitability of the coal and oil industries would encourage. Nothing would seem more counterproductive than to insist that the oil and gas companies invest only in the oil and gas industries.

When the potential but as yet undemonstrated dangers of horizontal integration are weighed against its proved advantages, there would seem to be little reason for concern. Movement toward higher levels of horizontal integration may merit close and continuing observation. However, at this point, it does not seem to justify legislation to restructure the energy industry by forcing horizontal divestiture.

---

13. Statement by the former Transportation Secretary before the Senate Antitrust and Monopoly Subcommittee, October 21, 1975 (mimeo).

CHAPTER SEVEN

Joint Ventures

Few practices in the oil industry have given rise to so much criticism, and so little research, as the widespread formation of joint ventures. Critics claim that concentration ratios and other measures of market power are of little use in measuring competition in the industry because of numerous joint venture arrangements. These arrangements effectively reduce the number of independent and self-motivated firms, they argue, because they provide a place where companies meet, exchange information and map out common strategies[1] On the other hand, others argue that joint ventures spread risk, promote efficiency and increase competition. One result of joint ventures, they contend, is lower prices to consumers.

Disagreement over the merits of joint ventures is hardly surprising. Ever since Cato the Elder first expressed doubts about the practice in 160 B.C.,[2] the competitive (or anticompetitive) significance of the joint venture has been the subject of considerable confusion. We do not pretend to have resolved this issue here. Instead, we simply review the various arguments advanced for and against joint venture in the oil industry. We also point out where the data and analysis necessary to assess the validity of these arguments are lacking.

---

1. See Wilson, John W. "Market Structure and Interfirm Integration in the Petroleum Industry." *Journal of Economic Issues,* Volume 9, 1975, pp. 319-335.

2. Cited in Machlup, Fritz, *The Political Economy of Monopoly.* Baltimore: Johns Hopkins University Press, 1952, pp. 185-86.

Probably the best formulation of the issues that one should consider in assessing the impact of joint ventures is provided by Walter Mead. Mead lists four basic justifications for joint venture operations:[3]

1. They permit entry into an industry or activity where absolute capital requirements are so high that only a few large firms could otherwise participate.
2. Risks may be so great that only a few, if any, existing firms would be willing to participate on their own.
3. Separate operations by competing firms may be economically inefficient.
4. In certain cases, large investments may produce external economies that will accrue to all firms regardless of their participation in the initial undertaking.

Mead also lists three possible drawbacks to joint ventures:[4]

1. Competition among horizontally-related firms may be restrained because the parents have a community of interests that discourages arm's length transactions.
2. Where the parents have a vertical relationship, market foreclosure may result because of preferred treatment toward the joint venture.
3. The parents may refrain from competing in the same market as the joint venture, thus reducing the total number of competitors in an industry.

In the oil industry a significant number of joint ventures occurs in offshore lease acquisition, exploratory and developmental drilling, ownership and production from oil and gas leases, pipeline ownership and operation, and international activities.[5] Because this book focuses on the domestic oil industry, we ignore international joint ventures.[6] We also defer the discussion of pipeline joint ventures to the next chapter.

Joint ventures are widely used in exploration and production of crude oil. Wilson has found that only four of the sixteen largest companies with interests in federal offshore leases produce more than 50 percent of their leases independently.[7] For the period 1954 through 1967, Mead has determined that, of the 20 largest oil companies, 14 were involved in joint venture arrangements.[8] From findings like these, critics have concluded that joint ventures are anticompetitive.

---

3. Mead, Walter J. "The Competitive Significance of Joint Ventures." *Antitrust Bulletin,* Volume 12, 1967, pp. 823-4.

4. *Ibid.,* pp. 822-3.

5. Duchesneau p. 48; John W. Wilson, *et al.,* "A Preliminary Report on the Market Structure and Competitive Features of the U.S. Petroleum Industry," unpublished paper submitted to the National Science Foundation, 1975, p. 17.

However, the mere existence of joint ventures, by itself, is not persuasive evidence of anticompetitive behavior. Proponents of the view that joint ventures are anticompetitive must go beyond merely presenting data on the existence of joint ventures; they must provide convincing evidence that the joint ventures have, in fact, been anticompetitive in intent or effect. As Duchesneau states, "It is. . .a leap of faith to conclude that the prevalence of joint ventures in oil and natural gas results in monopolization."[9]

In exploration and production, joint venture arrangements range from geological and seismic work on unexplored structures to the development of pilot projects to solve the unique drilling and production problems posed by operations in remote areas like Alaska and the North Sea. However, of the many kinds of joint venture arrangements in exploration and production, only one has been studied by policy analysts: joint bidding for oil and gas leases in Alaska and offshore.

Mead has found a tendency for companies bidding jointly on certain tracts at a sale not to bid against each other on the remaining tracts.[10] There is also a tendency for bidding partners at one sale to refrain from bidding against one another in other sales in the same area. However, this tendency disappears after about two years. Finally, Mead has found no tendency for those bidding together in

6. There is substantial evidence that, in the past, international joint ventures were anticompetitive. See Adelman, Morris. *The World Petroleum Market.* Baltimore: Johns Hopkins Press, 1972, pp. 86-8, and U.S. Senate, Select Committee on Small Business, *The International Petroleum Cartel,* Staff Report to the Federal Trade Commission, 82nd Cong., 2nd Sess., Comm. Print, 1952. See, also, Senate Committee on Foreign Relations, *Multinational Oil Coporations and U.S. Foreign Policy,* pp. 33-74; and Wilkins, Mira. "The Oil Companies in Perspective." *Daedalus,* Fall 1975, pp. 159-178. Such consortia as Aramco and the Anglo-Iranian Oil Company at one time effectively policed production and stabilized prices of foreign crude. Two things should be noted, however. First, these consortia were monopsonists with regard to producing countries. They had an incentive to keep the prices paid to producing countries as low as possible. For this reason, their interests were not necessarily opposed to those of U.S. consumers. Second, whatever monopsony power these foreign joint ventures enjoyed has now been completely eroded. The OPEC cartel is firmly in control of much of the foreign oil market and has assumed the market functions formerly performed by the international oil companies. Of course OPEC's objectives differ from those of the companies.

7. Testimony of John Wilson, *Hearings on the Natural Gas Industry Before the Subcommittee on Antitrust and Monopoly of the Senate Judiciary Committee,* 93rd Cong., 1st Sess., pt. 1, 1972, p. 482.

8. Mead, Walter J. "The Structure of the Buyer Market for Oil Shale Resources." *Natural Resources Journal,* Volume 8, October 1968, p. 618.

9. Duchesneau, p. 61.

10. Mead, "The Competitive Significance of Joint Ventures," pp. 838-46.

one geographic area to avoid bidding against each other in other areas.

Markham argues that joint bidding has actually increased competition among potential producers by adding to rather than subtracting from the total number of bidders on an individual tract.[11] Consistent with this finding, Markham also notes a tendency for joint bidding to be used more often by small and medium-sized firms rather than large firms.[12] Finally, Markham has developed a model to predict the expected sale price of a tract. He reasons that bids below the expected price would indicate collusion among bidders. Instead, Markham finds that companies have paid more than the expected price, a conclusion that leads him to reject the hypothesis of collusion in offshore lease sales.[13]

More recently, Mead has assembled data on the number of bidders per tract and the rate of return on OCS leases.[14] He begins with the hypothesis that fewer bidders per lease and an abnormally high rate of return might indicate the presence of anticompetitive behavior. He finds that the average number of bidders per tract has increased over time and that the average after tax rate of return on OCS tracts was only 6 percent during the period covered by his study. Mead thus concludes that, "joint biddings for outer continental shelf oil and gas leases pose no net threat to competition."

Finally, the Federal Trade Commission staff has just completed a comprehensive review and analysis of federal energy land policy. Although the staff did not directly address the issue of competition and joint bidding, its report includes a thorough analysis of the market for offshore oil and gas leases. It concludes that, "the market appears . . . to be effectively competitive. We have found no evidence of collusion [among bidders]."[15]

Yet, despite these findings, there has been considerable concern

11. Markham, Jesse W. "The Competitive Effects of Joint Bidding by Oil Companies for Offshore Leases." Markham and Papanek, eds. *Industrial Organization and Economic Development*. Boston: Houghton Mifflin, 1970, pp. 122-133.

12. Susan Wilcox has reached a similiar conclusion. See "Entry and Joint Venture Bidding in the Offshore Petroleum Industry." Ph.D. dissertation, University of California, Santa Barbara, 1974, p. 75.

13. Using a somewhat more sophisticated model, Erickson and Spann have reached the same conclusion. See Erickson, Edward and Spann, Robert. "The U.S. Petroleum Industry," Erickson and Waverman, eds. *The Energy Question: An International Failure of Policy*. Toronto: University of Toronto Press, Volume 2, 1974, pp. 14-17.

14. Statement of Walter Mead, *Hearings on Market Performance and Competition in the Petroleum Industry*, pt. 3, pp. 1005-1014.

over possible collusion among major oil companies bidding for OCS leases. Responding to this concern, the Department of Interior has issued regulations barring joint bidding among companies with average daily production of crude oil and natural gas in excess of 1.6 million barrels.[16] The Department has accepted the view that joint bidding among large firms reduces competition for leases and therefore the government's sale price.

This is thought to occur in two ways. First, because large firms are financially capable of submitting solo bids, joint bidding simply subtracts from the total number of bids that would otherwise be offered. Second, large firms, by discussing possible joint bid agreements with other companies prior to the sale, learn of the other companies' strategy and are able to adjust their own bids accordingly.[17]

Because of the attention that has been given to joint bidding in lease sales, one might assume that this type of joint venture is the most anitcompetitive. In fact, many critics of joint ventures believe that joint bidding is actually the least anticompetitive. For one thing, a joint bidding venture is short-lived. There is not the time to develop the community of interest believed to be so detrimental to a competitive environment. Also, the large amounts of money "left on the table" at lease sales suggest a lack of collusion or information exchanges by companies.

We know of no systematic studies of the competitive effects of joint venture agreements in exploratory and developmental drilling. However, it is clear that at least two real benefits accrue from them. First, because of economies of scale in these activities, individual efforts, particularly in the more remote areas, would be highly inefficient. More important, these joint ventures reduce the

---

15. Federal Trade Commission, Bureaus of Competition and Economics. *Report to the Federal Trade Commission on Federal Energy Land Policy: Efficiency, Revenue, and Competition.* October 1975, p. 359.

16. *Oil and Gas Journal.* October 6, 1975, p. 54. These regulations were originally issued at the Secretary of the Interior's discretion. They are now required by law. See Section 105 of the Energy Policy and Conservation Act of 1975.

17. Department of the Interior, Bureau of Land Management, Office of OCS Program Coordination, "An Analysis of the Proposed Ban on Joint Bidding," unpublished, June 1975. For an account of what is actually discussed in the preparation of joint bids see Gremillion, Charles C. "Offshore Leases in the Gulf of Mexico—Joint Venture Agreements and Related Matters." *25th Annual Oil and Gas Institute.* Matthew Bender Co., 1974, pp. 209-211. See Hughart, David. "Information Asymmetry, Bidding Stategies, and the the Marketing of Offshore Petroleum Leases." *Journal of Political Economy,* Volume 83, 1975, pp. 969-985 for a demonstration of how superior information can aid a bidder in devising an optimal strategy.

extraordinary risks inherent in the search for oil and gas. Only a small fraction of exploratory wells yield commercial finds of oil and gas. One way companies spread the risk of a dry hole, and also share the benefits of a find, is to enter into joint exploration ventures. The alternative to joint ventures would be higher prices to consumers in order to compensate for the higher risks of a single company venture.[18]

However, there is little risk in production. Why, then, do the oil companies enter into joint ventures in production? Another name for a joint venture in production is unitization of a reservoir, a widely supported method of conservation.[19] Its purpose is to prevent excessive drilling of production wells and to prevent the wasteful and too rapid exploitation of a reservoir. Cooperation in production assures maximum ultimate recovery. This cooperation, especially if it extends to decisions about output and marketing, may have anticompetitive overtones. Yet, when one weighs its benefits against its costs to society, it is hard to argue against unitization.[20]

The existence of collusive behavior in these types of joint ventures has probably been greatly exaggerated. However, what is needed is more analysis like that done on OCS bidding. For example, how does a community of interest in joint production arrangements manifest itself? Are there any patterns of behavior from which one might infer collusion or conspiracy? What kind of data are necessary to determine whether drilling joint ventures permit important social benefits? In short, until the argument that joint ventures are anticompetitive is more sharply drawn and the evidence supporting it is more specific, unsubstantiated rhetoric will continue to dominate the debate.

---

18. The relationship between risk and profits has long been accepted in economic theory. For a study which establishes this relationship empirically, see Fisher, I.N. and Hall, G.R. "Risk and Corporate Rates of Return." *Quarterly Journal of Economics*, Volume 73, February, 1969, pp. 79-92.

19. For the benefits of unit operation of a reservoir see Lovejoy, Wallace and Homan, Paul. *Economic Aspects of Oil Conservation Regulation.* Baltimore: Johns Hopkins Press, 1967, pp. 62-8 and McDonald, Stephen. *Petroleum Conservation in the United States.* Baltimore: Johns Hopkins Press. 1971, pp. 201-9.

20. *Ibid.,* pp. 145-6.

CHAPTER EIGHT

Pipelines

There are over 250 pipeline companies in the United States moving crude oil, light hydrocarbons and refined products. Of these companies, about a hundred are regulated by the Interstate Commerce Commission; the remainder are, for the most part, under the jurisdiction of state regulatory bodies. About 50 of the hundred pipelines subject to ICC regulations are joint ventures owned by consortia of oil companies, railroads and various firms not otherwise engaged in the oil industry. Others are wholly-owned subsidiaries of vertically integrated oil companies. On the whole, there is no predominant pattern of ownership in the pipeline industry.

Opponents of oil company ownership of pipelines generally voice two basic objections. First, because many pipelines are part of a vertically integrated operation, ownership of a pipeline by a refiner/producer or a refiner/marketer permits various forms of anticompetitive behavior already discussed in Chapter 4. Second, pipeline joint ventures involve close collaboration of companies that would otherwise compete at arm's length. It is alleged that this tends to limit competition in the same way as joint ventures in the exploration and production of crude oil.

Other objections to oil company involvement in pipelines have been raised by the Federal Trade Commission staff. In particular, the FTC staff has claimed that, because virtually all crude oil passes through pipelines owned in whole or in part by oil companies, the companies are able to control the distribution of crude oil and the output of independent refiners. The integrated oil companies are also able to exert considerable leverage on independent producers and marketers. As a result the independents' competitive position has been eroded. The FTC staff has also alleged that oil companies owning pipelines have manipulated tariff rates to their own advantage and to the disadvantage of competing modes of transportation. Finally, the staff has charged that the oil companies enjoy an unfair advantage through their ownership of pipelines because, in effect, they receive a rebate of pipeline tariff rates in the form of dividends.[1]

Criticism of the oil companies' ownership of pipelines is not new. Throughout the twentieth century there has been a recurring controversy over divorcement of pipelines from other segments of the oil industry.[2] Nearly thirty years ago, Eugene V. Rostow declared, "The chief weapon of the major companies for protecting their position is their ownership of pipelines."[3] In 1967, the U.S. Attorney General reported:

> The entire crude oil pipeline system is so dominated by the integrated companies that virtually all shipments, even if handled at origin or near destination by one of the few independent lines, must have intermediate access to an integrated company line. And outsiders simply are unable to use these lines as they could other types of common carriers.[4]

Objections to major oil company ownership of pipelines are essentially the same today as they were in the past. How valid are these objections?

For the nation as a whole, the pipelines are a relatively unconcentrated industry. The top four interstate pipelines control only 23 percent of the market; the top eight, only 42 percent.[5] However, critics charge that these data are misleading. In any one region crude oil and product pipelines are usually local monopolies. Only one pipeline generally serves a field or a group of refineries. The reason: economies of scale. It is often inefficient for two competing lines to operate side by side. (However, there are instances where pipelines have been laid parallel to each other, and experienced pipeliners, with whom we have spoken, have asserted that someone familiar with the system is often able to circumvent any local monopoly that might exist.)

---

1. FTC Staff, *Complaint Counsel's Prediscovery Statement,* pp. 67-8 and 82.

2. See Johnson, Arthur M. *Petroleum Pipelines and Public Policy: 1906-1959.* Cambridge: Harvard University Press, 1967.

3. Rostow, *A National Policy for the Oil Industry,* p. 57.

4. Cited in *Report,* p. S16403.

5. Statement of W.T. Slick, Vice President of Exxon, *Hearings on the Industrial Reorganization Act,* pt. 9, p. 451.

The pipelines have been treated as common carriers by the federal government since the beginning of this century. The real issue confronting public policy makers now is not whether the pipelines should be regulated as public utilities, but whether existing regulations are adequate.

In 1906 Congress passed the Hepburn Act which declared pipelines in interstate trade to be common carriers and required these lines to transport oil brought to them from any source at fair and reasonable terms. The pipelines were also placed under the jurisdiction of the Interstate Commerce Commission and were prohibited from discriminating among different users of the same line.

After passage of the Hepburn Act, some pipeline companies claimed they were not common carriers because they served only their own facilities. In 1912, the ICC held that the Congress had intended to regulate these pipelines as well. In the ensuing Pipelines Cases, the Supreme Court upheld the Commission. Subsequently, the courts established that a pipeline owned by one oil company transporting only that company's oil can be treated as a common carrier for reporting purposes, but is not required to carry oil for other companies or to have its rates approved by the ICC. However, joint venture pipelines were declared common carriers and were required to transport oil for non-owners under nondiscriminatory terms.

The pipelines are also covered by the Elkins Act of 1903 which disallows rebates and other forms of discrimination by common carriers. On the basis of this act, in 1941 the Justice Department brought suit against 41 pipeline companies alleging that dividends paid to these companies were, in effect, an illegal rebate that discriminated against non-owner users of the pipelines. This litigation resulted in a consent decree allowing shipper-owners of common carrier pipelines to receive dividends of no more than 7 percent of the valuation of the pipelines' property, this valuation to be determined by the ICC. Earnings above this rate must be put in a special fund earmarked, primarily, for new construction and retirement of debt.

There have been other complaints about the integrated oil companies' pipelines since passage of the Hepburn Act. As a rule, these complaints have been resolved satisfactorily by the ICC or the courts.

For example, it was found that the maintenance of high minimum tender requirements (or minimum shipment levels) prevented small oil producers and refiners from shipping oil in trunklines owned by the large, integrated companies. In 1922, the ICC lowered minimum tender requirements from 100,000 to 10,000 barrels and subsequently reaffirmed this level and its right to establish minimum tenders in various cases brought before it. Today, not only does the ICC determine the minimum tender, it can require prorationing of a pipeline's capacity among all users in the event that this capacity is fully utilized.

The pipeline companies were also accused of maintaining excessively high rates in order to depress the price of oil paid to independent producers and to squeeze the profits of independent refiners. In the 1930's the ICC investigated pipeline rates and found that the rates of some companies had, indeed, been excessive.Since then, the Commission has established even more firmly its power to regulate rates charged by the interstate common carrier pipelines.[6]

Most intrastate pipelines are also regulated as common carriers by the states. In fact, many states had declared pipelines to be common carriers prior to passage of the Hepburn Act in 1906, and at least twenty states regulated interstate pipelines as common carriers as early as 1890. In short, the pipelines are already extensively regulated by federal and state governments. The relevant question is: Is this regulation enough?

In attempting to answer this question, the Chairman of the ICC recently told Congress that, "Today there are so few complaints and so few problems that I must say [the pipelines are] one of the best run transportation systems we have."[7] He went on to state:

> In conclusion, it would appear that except for certain impediments brought about because of environmental considerations pipelines have been constructed on an as-needed basis and generally provide good service. It has been our experience that pipeline rates are just and reasonable . . . . We have received no complaints in recent years involving allegations relative to the size of tender, the failure to publish through routes and joint rates, or to provide service to independents.[8]

Although the pipeline companies can probably find subtle ways of discriminating against non-owner users, the ICC is a forum to which these users can take their complaints. This is, perhaps, its most important role in maintaining competition in the pipeline industry.

Sometimes even the threat of suit is enough to prevent discriminatory actions on the part of major oil company owners of

---

6. The foregoing discussion draws heavily on Johnson, Arthur, *Petroleum Pipelines,* and Testimony of the Honorable George Stafford, Chairman of the ICC, *Hearings on Market Performance,* pt. 3, pp. 875-913. See, also, Statement of Jack Vickery, *Hearings on the Consumer Energy Act of 1974,* pt. 2, pp. 620-623.

7. Testimony of the Honorable George Stafford, p. 896.

8. *Ibid.,* p. 901.

pipelines. For example, a recent Senate Antitrust Committee staff report critical of oil company ownership of pipelines quotes testimony by the president of APCO, a small refiner.[9] APCO had bid away crude oil produced by an independent in Texas from SUNOCO, the producer's previous customer. According to APCO's president, Sun Pipeline advised his company that it could not move its newly acquired crude oil on the pipeline because it did not meet vapor specifications, even though the line had previously moved the same crude oil when it had belonged to SUNOCO. APCO threatened to sue. A few hours later, Sun Pipeline agreed to transport APCO's crude. Although the staff report presents this case as an example of a pipeline company abuse, it is really an example of how well the system works. As it turned out, APCO was protected by the law.

The ICC has received relatively few complaints about exclusionary practices by pipeline companies.[10] Since 1969, the Commission has considered only 18 cases protesting pipeline tariffs.[11] To some industry critics, the reason there are so few complaints is that independent companies fear retaliation by the majors. Yet, many of these same independents have been highly vocal in opposition to the major oil companies on other issues, such as petroleum allocation and entitlements. Where their basic interests are at stake the independents have been anything but reticent.

There is no evidence of discriminatory behavior by the pipelines toward independent producers. In fact, about 4,000 independent oil and natural gas producers have, through their trade association, The Independent Petroleum Association of America, stated on several occasions that they have *not* been denied access to major oil company owned pipelines. In a letter sent to each United States Senator on July 12, 1973, Tom B. Medders, Jr., then President of the IPAA, said, "This is to advise you that we are not aware of any producer having difficulty selling or moving his crude oil, and we do not believe any such discrimination exists."[12] Another letter dated November 6, 1973, from Dan Jones, General Counsel to the IPAA, to Senator Stevenson said, "The conclusion that independent producers may have difficulty securing shipment of their oil, and are subject to discrimination by pipeline companies, is not supported by the experience of independent producers."[13]

---

9. Cited in *Report*, p. S16405.
10. Letter from Hon. George M. Stafford to Hon. Joe L. Evins, reprinted in *Hearings on the Consumer Energy Act of 1974*, pt. 2, pp. 641-643.
11. *Hearings on the Industrial Reorganization Act*, pt. 9, pp. 653-4.
12. Reproduced in *Hearings on the Consumer Energy Act of 1974*, pt. 2, p. 711.
13. *Ibid.*, pp. 597-598.

A recent tabulation by the Association of Oil Pipe Lines, based on information provided by 51 pipeline companies accounting for most of the petroleum products shipped by pipeline in the United States, found that most shippers were non-owners. Of a total of 909 shippers on these lines, only 103 owned all or part of them. Moreover, of the 806 non-owner shippers, only 233 were major oil companies. The rest were independents.[14]

Critics of the industry have also charged that major oil company ownership of pipelines has put other competing forms of transportation, particularly tankers, at a competitive disadvantage. The integrated oil companies own tankers as well as pipelines. The reason they may prefer pipelines is that these lines are usually the least cost method of transporting crude oil and refined products. A major reason for this is the Jones Act which requires that goods transported in the U. S. coastal trade be carried on relatively high cost U. S. flag tankers. This "gift" to the U. S. maritime industry and unions has helped to undermine the competitive viability of tanker transport of oil in the United States. Once again, the culprit has been the government, not the monopolistic oil industry.

There have been charges that the pipelines, especially those that are jointly owned, have earned excessive profits. In fact, a thorough study of pipeline company profits in 1971 by Stewart Myers of the Massachusetts Institute of Technology has found no evidence that the pipeline companies' rate of return on investment has been out of line.[15] In fact, this study determined that the average rate of return for the pipeline industry was about the same as that for A.T. & T. even though the pipelines are probably exposed to greater risk.

Critics have been especially concerned with the anticompetitive implications of joint venture pipelines. The staff of the Senate Antitrust and Monopoly Subcommittee states:

Regardless of the legality of any specific trunk line the total effect must contribute substantially to restraining competition. The construction and operation of such lines inevitably involves a sharing of information about the partner's intentions and capabilities in crude production.[16]

Congress has also been concerned with how joint venture partners are selected, what is discussed at the preliminary meetings, and what type of information is exchanged between participants.[17]

14. Letter from Association of Oil Pipe Lines to Hon. Warren Magnuson, *Hearings on the Consumer Energy Act of 1974*, pt. 2, pp. 665-6.

15. Testimony by Stewart C. Myers, *Market Performance and Competition in the Petroleum Industry*, pt. 5, p. 1648.

16. *Report*, p. S16405.

17. For example, see *Hearings on the Industrial Reorganization Act*, pt. 9, pp. 625-627.

Information pertaining to the operation of joint venture pipelines is protected by ICC regulations. The pipeline companies are prohibited from disclosing the throughput of any pipeline user to anyone, even an owner of the pipeline, and, in actual practice, the operating and planning divisions of major oil company pipeline owners are restricted in their contact with pipeline personnel. All requests for information typically go to a single corporate officer who is usually the corporation's representative on the pipeline company's board.

Obviously, in the planning of a new pipeline venture, or in the expansion of an existing line, some information about future plans passes among corporations. But how much information passes? How valuable is it to competitors? And, how could this information impede competition?

In short, it is difficult to make a case for further regulation of the pipeline industry. Existing regulations appear adequate to protect against anticompetitive abuse. Nor has a case been made for the divestiture of the integrated oil companies' holdings in pipelines or the break-up of joint ventures in the pipeline industry. The likely outcome of actions against the pipelines will be disruption and confusion in the oil industry, precisely what the nation does not need nor should it want at this time.

According to critics of the industry, the ICC is ineffective in enforcing existing regulations and, as a result, the pipelines have been guilty of monopolistic abuses. The proposed remedy: more regulations and even divestiture. What seems odd, however, is that those who are supposedly suffering at the hands of the pipelines do not seem to be objecting to their treatment. It is difficult to find someone who has been abused. One is reminded of Othello's complaint: "I swear 'tis better to be much abus'd than but to know't a little."

CHAPTER NINE

Exchange and Processing Agreements

Two other practices by the oil industry similar to joint ventures have also been singled out by critics as potentially anticompetitive. These are exchange and processing agreements.

Exchange agreements serve several functions. One is to assure that refiners obtain the types of crude oil they need. For example, a large, integrated company may produce several hundred distinct types of crude oil. Yet, its refineries may be designed to run only half of them. One way to consolidate crude oils so that they have the proper gravity, sulfur content, and other quality specifications is the mechanism of exchange. Without exchange in one form or another, the refiner would have to make substantial and essentially wasteful investments in plant and equipment.

Exchange agreements are also, in effect, a highly efficient form of transportation. Rather than ship crude oil and refined products long distances, both integrated and independent oil companies have found it mutually beneficial to swap oil among themselves. A skilled crude and product trader is one of the most valued employees of an oil company. Using only a telephone, he is often able to "move" crude from Texas to California or product from Seattle to Bangor in a few hours. And, if he is exceptionally skilled, he is able to do this at minimal cost to his company. Exchange agreements are widely used for both crude oil and refined products. Because of these agreements, a significant share of the crude oil refined by an integrated company may actually come from other producers or owners, while a significant share of the product sold by the company may come from other refiners.

Processing agreements are less common. Under these agreements, oil companies pay others to refine their oil. Most processing agreements involve newly built refining capacity. A refiner's capacity is often expanded in discrete jumps because of economies of large scale operations. To make full use of capacity until marketing operations also expand, refiners will agree to process crude oil owned by others for a specified period of time. While exchange agreements are a means of transporting oil as little as possible, processing agreements are a means of utilizing refining capacity as efficiently as possible. Both types of agreements benefit consumers by permitting lower prices.

Yet both types of agreements have been under attack for being inherently anti-competitive. For example, the staff of the Federal Trade Commission has alleged that exchange agreements effectively deny independent refiners access to crude oil and exclude potential new entrants from refining and marketing. The staff also argues that these agreements facilitate price fixing throughout a market area, increase effective concentration in both marketing and refining, and permit the integrated companies to avoid open market sales. Exchange agreements, the staff claims, raise costs to consumers because they are barter arrangements involving misallocation of society's scarce resources.[1] Others have charged that exchange agreements are used to avoid public regulation of pipelines, to deny the true value of crude oil to producers, to cheat royalty owners, and to avoid paying state and local taxes.[2]

Similarly, processing agreements are accused of having given the majors *de facto* control over portions of the independent refiners' capacity and, in this way, effectively increasing concentration in refining. Also, it is alleged that refiners blessed with processing agreements generally avoid selling products to particularly aggressive independent marketers. Thus, processing agreements diminish competition at both the refining and marketing levels of the industry.[3]

Exchange agreements would be anticompetitive if some companies, by engaging in them, were able to exclude from the marketplace other companies unable to obtain supplies of crude oil and products from alternative sources. Exchange agreements might also help to stabilize market-sharing arrangements among major oil companies.[4] Two questions should be posed, however. First, have

---

1. FTC Staff, *Complaint Counsel's Prediscovery Statement,* pp. 53, 56, and 88. Also, FTC Staff, *Preliminary Report,* p. 30.

2. See California Legislature, Joint Committee on Public Domain, "Crude Oil Exchanges: The Other Currency," September 1974, esp. pp. 11 and 26-29.

3. FTC Staff, *Complaint Counsel's Prediscovery Statement,* p. 36.

these abuses actually occurred? And second, even if they have, do the gains in efficiency resulting from exchange and processing agreements more than offset the loss of competition in the marketplace?

The staff of the Senate Antitrust and Monopoly Subcommittee argues that exchange and processing agreements have, in fact, been used to suppress competition.

> Some of this activity is clearly cooperative and probably quite anticompetitive in nature. . .The most important cooperative device in refinery operation is the exchange agreement. The net effect. . .is the elimination of any kind of free market either for raw materials going into the refineries or for product coming out.[5]

The staff also argues that the assertion made by the companies that exchange agreements eliminate unnecessary movement of oil is a "straw man." The alternative to exchange agreements, it contends, is buying and selling in open markets.[6] In addition, the staff claims that the barrel-for-barrel terms of exchange agreements eliminate price competition, in effect, by eliminating price. For these reasons, the staff argues, exchange and processing agreements put the small refiners in a dependent position relative to the major oil companies.[7]

Apparently, the staffs of the Federal Trade Commission and the Senate Antitrust Subcommittee accept the argument first put forward by DeChazeau and Kahn that exchange agreements may benefit only the integrated oil companies.[8] DeChazeau and Kahn note that, for an exchange to take place, there must be both a need for a particular crude oil at a particular place and possession of crude oil either at a different place or of a different type. In other words, companies involved in exchanges must control crude oil at both the production and refining levels. For this reason, independent refiners without crude are unable to share in the benefits which result from exchange agreements.

The various critics of exchange agreements are wrong in asserting that no price, either implicit or explicit, is involved in exchanges and that oil is swapped under exchange agreements on a

---

4. Statement by Steven Breyer, *Market Performance and Competition in the Petroleum Industry*, pt. 1, p. 446.

5. *Report*, p. S16405.

6. *Ibid.*, p. S16405.

7. *Ibid.*, S16406; see, also, FTC Staff, *Complaint Counsel's Prediscovery Statement*, p. 88.

8. DeChazeau and Kahn, pp. 185-6.

barrel-for-barrel basis. In fact, oil traded on a barrel-for-barrel basis is the exception, not the rule. There are quality and transportation differentials for crude oil which are reflected in the prices at which it is traded. There are also quality and transportation differentials for refined products and, in some instances, different types of refined products are swapped between companies. It is not uncommon, for example, for a company to trade gasoline for home heating oil when its refinery yields do not correspond to its market needs. Under these circumstances, bartering of oil is not only infrequent, it is virtually impossible. Exchange agreements are usually written in terms of prices. These prices may be posted prices for crude oil or market prices for products. Invariably, these prices are negotiated by the trading partners.

Posted prices tend to be used in continuing exchange relationships. Some critics have charged, however, that posted prices are themselves a result of anticompetitive behavior in the industry.[9] Purchasers rather than producers of crude oil have historically set posted prices. This is correct. However, in the absence of federal allocation regulations, producers are free to sell to other refiners. (Witness the Sun Pipeline case discussed in Chapter 8.) It was the producers' ability to switch from one purchaser to another that led to the sharp increase in posted prices for unregulated oil in mid-1973. The evidence suggests a competitive market for domestic crude oil in which the producers, not the major oil company purchasers, have recently been in a strong competitive position.

The market for oil has been heavily influenced by the government's price controls. Under the two-tier price system, which was in force from August 1973 until February 1976, the price of so-called "old" oil was subject to a ceiling, while "new," "released," and "stripper" crudes were unregulated. All but one of the 17 largest oil companies is crude deficient.[10] To the extent that old oil has been purchased from independent producers by the integrated refiners, the effect of the two-tier system was to depress posted prices. However, the companies can hardly be faulted for being anticompetitive. The real culprit is, once again, the government's price controls.[11]

In preparing this chapter, we have talked with officials of a

---

9. See California Legislature, Joint Committee on Public Domain, pp. 1-12.

10. See Table 11.

11. The Energy Policy and Conservation Act of 1975 has mandated several changes in crude oil price regulations. What the final regulations will be is unclear as of this writing. However, some form of two- or multi-tier system will remain, with ceilings put on the prices of all domestic oil, whether produced by the integrated oil companies or independent producers.

number of oil companies. All major oil companies with whom we have spoken have made crude trades with independent refiners and producers within the past year. They have also made product trades with independent as well as major oil company refiners. The attitude among the major oil company officials was a willingness to trade with anybody as long as the price was right and the oil was of the proper type and quality. Similarly, all small refiners queried have made trades with major oil companies, and those who wished to trade but did not possess any crude oil of their own have usually been able to purchase the crude necessary to make exchanges. None expressed substantial displeasure with the treatment now received from their major oil company trading partners.[12]

The same is true of processing agreements. These agreements are by no means an exclusive practice of the integrated oil companies, as critics have implied. Such independent refiners as Crown Central and Amerada Hess have processed crude oil supplied to them by major oil companies. The crucial factor is whether a company's refining capacity exceeds its marketing capacity. If so, it is likely to seek arrangements to process crude oil for other companies to keep its refinery capacity fully utilized.

In most instances, exchange and processing agreements have not been anticompetitive. This is not to say that these agreements will, under all circumstances, be free of competitive abuses. Occasionally, abuses may occur.

An example of a processing agreement that was alleged to be anticompetitive in effect, if not intent, and which received widespread criticism was an arrangement between Texaco and Coastal States in 1973. Texaco contracted with Coastal States, an independent refiner, to process 14,000 bpd of crude oil initially. Under this agreement, Coastal States was to refine successively greater amounts of Texaco's crude oil over a ten-year period. Texaco planned to market the refined product through its own retail outlets. However, following this agreement, Coastal States cut off the supplies of some of its own independent customers. Critics alleged that the purpose of this arrangement was not to utilize Coastal States' refining capacity more efficiently, but to enlarge Texaco's market share to the mutual advantage of Texaco and Coastal States and to the disadvantage of the independent marketers.

In fact, under the processing agreement, the amount of crude oil Coastal States would have refined for Texaco initially was well below

---

12. There were complaints several years ago. However, the major reason for the inability of some independent refiners to swap crude oil with the major oil companies was the Cost of Living Council's regulations and shortages created by the Arab oil embargo: see Chapter 4.

the amount of idle capacity at Coastal States' refinery. Moreover, Coastal States was supposed to expand its refinery to meet the additional requirements of Texaco in the future. There was no reason why the agreement should have reduced supplies to Coastal States' existing customers.

This processing agreement had two major consequences. First, it created a highly negative impression on many congressmen in whose districts Coastal States' independent customers resided. The processing agreement was one of several reasons for the overwhelming support for passage of the Emergency Petroleum Allocation Act in November 1973. To the congressmen, the agreement provided a tangible example of how big oil companies were hurting little oil companies. Second, the Justice Department brought suit against Texaco and Coastal States on the grounds that the processing agreement was anticompetitive in fact if not in intent. In January 1974 the case was settled by consent decree. Coastal States was allowed to process for Texaco up to 45,000 bpd or 25 percent of its refinery capacity, whichever is lower. The decree, in effect, sustained most of the processing agreement but, at the same time, protected Coastal States' existing customers' supplies.[13]

Perhaps the most important outcome of this litigation was that all systems worked. Existing antitrust law was sufficient to protect Coastal States' independent customers. Moreover, the processing agreement, as a practice, was essentially vindicated by the Justice Department. The problems faced by the independent marketers did not result from the agreement *per se,* but the fact that Coastal States chose, for one reason or another, to alter its marketing system at the time the agreement was enacted.

Exchange and processing agreements provide flexibility in the refining and distribution of oil. They avoid cross-hauling and duplication of refinery capacity and, in this way, enable lower costs of production and distribution. They also reduce the need for new transport and terminal facilities and thus reduce the impact of crude oil operations on the environment. For this reason, the California Coastal Zone Conservation Commission has actually recommended that oil companies be encouraged to engage in exchange agreements.[14]

Several observers would replace exchange and processing agreements with a crude oil and product market.[15] However, these

---

13. *United States v. Texaco, et al.,* CCH 1973-2 Trade Cases 1, Par. 74,831.

14. *Platt's Oilgram,* December 3, 1975. Ironically, the Joint Committee on Public Domain of the California Legislature has condemned exchange agreements as detrimental to the interests of the State. See note 9 above.

15. For example, see Statement of Stephen Breyer, p. 446. See, also, *Report,* p. S16405.

observers apparently fail to realize that a market already exists. Exchange and processing agreements are market transactions. If a law were passed prohibiting these agreements, but permitting market transactions, little change in existing practice would be necessary other than adopting a new name for it. If, however, the law were written to exclude all forms of exchange, whether by barter or for money, the consequences could be very serious indeed. Then, American consumers would be required to pay higher prices reflecting the higher cost of refining and distributing oil.

The result of such a law could also be greater concentration in refining and marketing in various regions of the country. This, in turn, could lead to less competition in the industry. The Tenth Circuit Court of Appeals noted this possibility in *Blue Bell Co. v. Frontier Refining Co.*[16] In its decision, the court pointed out that exchanges of refined products "permitted one marketing company to do business at the back door of its competitor's refinery. . ."[17] In the absence of exchange agreements, refiners would be forced to suspend marketing in certain regions of the country where their refining capacity is limited or non-existent. Refiners would also be unlikely to compete for crude oil in regions relatively distant from their refineries. In other words, exchange agreements may actually increase rather than lessen competition in the oil industry.

Instead of outlawing exchange and processing agreements we think it better to assess each agreement on a case-by-case basis to determine whether it violates existing anti-trust law. There is precedent for this type of approach to the problem. Case-by-case adjudication has formed the basis of our common law system for over 800 years.

---

16. 213 F.2d 354 (1954).
17. *Ibid.*, p. 359.

CHAPTER TEN

Interlocking Directorates

One of the ways the major oil companies are able to suppress competition, it is claimed, is through the existence of an extensive network of interlocking boards of directors. Critics argue that these interlocks "serve to reinforce mutual interests and provide an opportunity for reconciling differences and achieving intercorporate harmony."[1] In addition, because of interlocks between major oil companies and large banks, new firms are said to be unable to obtain financing for refineries and other capital intensive projects.[2]

Concern over the anticompetitive effects of interlocking directorates is not new. Nor has this concern been directed solely at the oil industry.[3] During the early part of the twentieth century several congressional committees and reform groups investigated this practice and found widespread abuses resulting from it. For example, in 1912 the Stanley Committee reported that interlocking directorates were responsible for inside deals, kickbacks, and illegal rebates.[4] As a result of this and other investigations, Congress

---

1. Wilson, John W. "Market Structure in the Petroleum Industry," p. 328.

2. FTC Staff, *Complaint Counsel's Prediscovery Statement,* pp. 19-21.

3. For a historical perspective, see Staff of the House of Committee on the Judiciary, 89th Cong., 1st Sess., *Report on Interlocks in Corporate Management,* Washington, D.C.: Government Printing Office, 1965; Travers, Arthur. "Interlocks in Corporate Management and the Antitrust Laws." *Texas Law Review.* Volume 46, July 1968, pp. 819-850.

4. *Investigation of United States Steel Corp.* House of Representatives Report No. 1127, 62nd Cong., 2nd Sess., August 1912, cited in House Judiciary Committee Staff, p. 4.

adopted Section 8 of the Clayton Act which prohibits any individual from serving on the boards of two or more competing firms.

But reformers have never been satisfied with Section 8 and for many years have advocated amendments that would strengthen it.[5] One of their major complaints is that Section 8 does not prohibit indirect interlocks.[6]

The staff of the House Judiciary Committee has identified three types of indirect interlocks.[7]

1. Board members from competing firms may sit on the board of a third company. For example, early in 1975 the chairmen of Exxon and Standard of Indiana were members of the board of the Chase Manhattan Bank.[8]

2. Board members of a third company may sit on the boards of competing firms. For example, in early 1975 directors from General Foods sat on the boards of Shell, Mobil and Gulf.[9]

3. Finally, directors from competing firms may occupy seats on the boards of companies that are, in turn, linked by a common board member.

How do indirect interlocks suppress competition? Some critics suggest that interlocks may be used as a channel for information which enables collusive behavior. The board room is believed to be a "safe house" where the chances of detection by law enforcement officials are slight. However, absent other more compelling evidence, it is difficult to condemn interlocks on this ground alone. Why would conspirators have to use the board rooms of third companies as a place in which to hatch illegal schemes? Oil industry executives can almost certainly find other, safer places in which to break the law. Indeed, the staff of the Federal Trade Commission asserts that the Petroleum Club in Houston serves just this purpose.[10] Even better, the oil companies might use organizations that do not have the words "oil" or "petroleum" in their names. To really insure against collusion, perhaps the government should ban membership by officials of more than one oil company in the same country club or church.

---

5. Most recently in H.R. 4406, which was introduced by Congressman Michael Harrington on March 8, 1975.

6. See, for example, letter from FTC Chairman Dixon to Congressman Manuel Cellar reprinted, in part, in House Judiciary Committee Staff, pp. 101-102.

7. House Judiciary Committee Staff, p. 10.

8. Keeler, Andrew G. *A Citizen's Oil Factbook: What Every Citizen Should Know About the Eighteen Largest Oil Companies.* Washington, D.C.: Center for Science in the Public Interest, 1975, pp. 19 and 34.

9. *Ibid.*, p. 8.

10. FTC Staff, *Complaint Counsel's Prediscovery Statement,* p. 48.

A second and more subtle way in which indirect interlocks may result in anticompetitive behavior is through manipulations by what C. Wright Mills has termed a "power elite." This elite, through service on the boards of different companies, could coordinate policies to prevent competition. The elite could also control the flow of credit by sitting on the boards of financial institutions. Angus McDonald claims that:

> Oil company directors who are directors of banks and other corporations form a cozy and exclusive club where it is convenient for them to reach understandings and agreements which result in common, if not conspiratorial, action. . . .Outsiders simply do not know what goes on behind the closed doors of the financial institutions. One can reasonably suspect that in times of tight money the independent oil companies, which do not have interlocked directorships with the major banks, would find it difficult to get financing.[11]

It is also thought that directors sitting on the board of a third company can influence the policies of that company to their own firm's mutual advantage.

Although considerable amounts of data have been collected on the existence of indirect interlocks involving the oil industry,[12] there has been little or no analysis of these data. The House Judiciary Committee staff observed in 1965 that, in comparison with other large firms, the oil companies have discouraged their directors and officers from serving on the boards of other corporations.[13] However, the staff went on to conclude:

> There is virtually no reliable current information available that will demonstrate either acceptable or undesirable effects that have resulted from the fact that common management personnel participated in, or influenced, particular business transactions. Without factual information concerning the actual operation of interlocks, "commonsense," presupposition, reliance on past proof, and abstract reasoning have been predominant in the analysis of both the virtues and evils attributed to corporate interlocks.[14]

There has been nothing since this report was issued in 1965 that would change its conclusion.[15] Analyses of the effects of interlocking

---

11. McDonald, Angus. *Interlocking Oil: Big Oil Ties with Other Corporations.* Washington, D.C.: Center for Science in the Public Interest, 1974, pp. 7-8.

12. For example, see Wilson, John, "Market Performance" and House Judiciary Committee Staff.

13. House Judiciary Committee Staff, pp. 120, 125 and 137.

14. *Ibid.,* p. 229.

15. Scherer reached the same conclusion in 1970. See Scherer, F.M., *Industrial Market Structure and Economic Performance.* Chicago: Rand McNally, 1970, p. 47.

directorates have never gone beyond the finding that they exist.

In our judgment, the issue is essentially irrelevant to a serious discussion of competition in the petroleum industry. The validity of the argument against interlocks turns on two crucial assumptions. First, it is assumed that the board of directors of a major company or financial institution actually controls the firm's policy. Second, it is assumed that interlocked directors, even though usually a minority on a company's board, will be able to impose their view on the other directors and the company's management. Also, implicit in these arguments is the view that interlocking directorates serve no useful purpose.

Practically every state corporation statute declares that "the business of the corporation shall be managed by the board of directors." However, most often this is not the case. True control is exercised either by the chairman and the president alone or by the chairman, president, and inside directors.[16] Outside directors usually do not have the time nor the expertise to contest management's policies. Instead, they act as mere advisors and consultants or as a sounding board for management's proposals.[17]

But, putting this argument aside, how likely is it that interlocking directors will be able to influence a company's policy? The answer: not very. In most companies outside directors are to be seen and not heard. "Professional courtesy" and "corporate manners" are the norm. Outside directors who ask management embarassing questions, let alone attempt to influence policy, often find that they are still outside but directors no more.[18] Interlocking directorates serve a useful purpose. Interlocks involving financial institutions, for example, provide expertise on financial matters. For this reason, directors and officers of major financial institutions are often preferred candidates for a board membership. By the same token, the expertise that an officer-director of an oil company possesses can also make him a valuable outside director.[19]

16. Mason, Edwards. "The Apologetics of Managerialism." *The Journal of Business,* January 1958, p. 1; House Judiciary Committee Staff, p. 230. Because of this fact, the staff of the Judiciary Committee argued that "interlocks of officers and other senior employees probably are of more consequence on matters of antitrust significance than are interlocks of directors," House Judiciary Committee Staff, pp. 230-1. However, we know of no one who has even considered this aspect of the problem with respect to the oil industry.

17. Mace, Myles L. *Directors: Myth and Reality.* Boston: Harvard Graduate School of Business Administration, 1971, pp. 43-68.

18. *Ibid.,* pp. 54-57.

19. *Ibid.,* pp. 13-23. Mace quotes the president of a medium-sized corporation as saying that he found advice by an oil industry executive on real estate matters especially valuable. The corporation president attributed this to the executive's experience in buying and leasing service stations throughout the nation.

Only a total cynic would believe that the purpose of all or even most interlocking directorates is to establish and exercise monopoly power. However, those who want to find a conspiracy in the oil industry usually succeed in convincing themselves that a conspiracy does in fact exist. No other argument that anticompetitive behavior exists in the oil industry seems so empty or so misanthropic.

CHAPTER ELEVEN

Barriers to Entry

One essential element of monopoly power is the ability to keep new firms from entering the market. In a competitive industry, as soon as firms begin to restrict output and earn monopoly profits, new firms, attracted by these profits, will penetrate the market. The result will be a return to competitive levels of profits. However, whether new firms will actually enter the market when profits are above normal depends on whether there are barriers to entry.

Critics claim that barriers to entry by new firms exist at all levels of the petroleum industry.[1] Without these barriers to entry, it is asserted, "existing excess profits would attract new firms which would increase supply at all levels and . . . eliminate the excess profits."[2] We leave the question of oil industry profitability to the next chapter. Here, we focus on the existence or nonexistence of barriers to entry.

There is no evidence of barriers to entry in onshore oil and gas exploration and production. Independents have always played an important role in exploration and production,[3] and state regulations on production have insured that, once a field is discovered, the independents will not be squeezed out by major producers.[4] Repeal

---

1. FTC Staff, *Preliminary Report,* p. 25.

2. *Ibid.,* p. 25.

3. See McKie, James W. "Market Structure and Uncertainty in Oil and Gas Exploration." *Quarterly Journal of Economics,* Volume 74, November 1960, pp. 546-554.

4. McKie, James W. and McDonald, Stephen L. "Petroleum Conservation in Theory and Practice." *Quarterly Journal of Economics,* Volume 76, February 1962, pp. 110-118.

of the depletion allowance for major producers will also help to insure a continued role for the smaller independents. Under the tax law changes:

> Some of the prospects rejected by the majors will remain attractive to independents retaining the depletion allowance, so the latter group will tend to expand operations (partly through new entrants), taking leases no longer competed for by majors. . .[5]

By contrast, there are greater barriers to entry in offshore oil and gas exploration and production. The cash bonus system for lease acquisition and the unlimited liability imposed on operators for oil spills are the two principal barriers identified in a survey conducted by the Independent Petroleum Association of America in 1971[6] Despite these barriers, however, Wilcox found 132 separate firms participating as winning bidders in the 33 OCS sales between October 1954 and March 1974.[7] Furthermore, several proposals have been advanced that would lower these barriers in the future. Under consideration in the Congress are various bills limiting liability for offshore spills to fixed sums.[8] The Federal Trade Commission Staff has also suggested an ingenious new bidding procedure for OCS leases that would reduce the cash bonus requirement and encourage exploration by independent firms.[9]

Based on our own discussions with industry executives at all levels, we have been unable to identify any significant entry barriers in marketing. Capital requirements are low, and often an integrated company or large jobber will provide financial and technical assistance to a potential entrant. The persistent growth in the market share of independents, discussed in Chapters 2 and 3, confirms this absence of major barriers to entry in the marketing sector.

In refining, however, there are substantial barriers to entry and, for this reason, most of the controversy has centered on the refining segment of the industry. Capital requirements are high; today, new refineries cost anywhere between $2,000 and $2,500 per barrel per day of capacity.[10] A new refinery also requires an assured supply of crude oil. With uncertainties in both the domestic and world crude

---

5. McDonald, "Taxation System and Market Distortion," p. 34

6. "Offshore Entry Baffles Independents." *Oil and Gas Journal.* December 6, 1971, p. 44.

7. Wilcox, p. 66.

8. For example, H.R. 9294 and H.R. 10363.

9. Federal Trade Commission, Bureaus of Economics and Competition, Chapter 12.

10. Hass, Jerome E., Mitchell, Edward J. and Stone, Bernell K. *Financing the Energy Industry.* Cambridge: Ballinger Publishing Company, 1974, p. 32.

market, obtaining a guaranteed supply is no easy task. Finally, even if the would-be entrant has obtained the necessary financial backing and crude supply, opposition from local and environmental groups may prevent construction of a refinery. These groups have managed to block the construction of at least 16 new refineries during the past several years.[11]

Not surprisingly, critics argue that the major oil companies have been primarily responsible for preventing firms from entering refining. The FTC staff charges that the majors "have consistently acted to erect and maintain" barriers to entry in refining. [12] Allvine and Patterson claim that, "since 1950 the integrated oil companies have taken over several of the important independent refineries and there have been built no new independent refineries with over 50,000 barrels per day capacity."[13]

The FTC staff lists a number of ways in which the majors have been able to keep new firms out of refining.[14] Through import quotas, market demand prorationing and the ownership and control of pipelines the majors have allegedly been able to deny a potential entrant an assured supply of crude oil. Through interlocking directorates between majors and large financial institutions, the majors have denied financing to would-be refiners. Finally, the staff alleges that, by their control of gasoline marketing, the majors have also kept independent firms from entering refining.

It is also argued that vertical integration itself is a barrier to entry.[15] Because most refiners are integrated, potential entrants will be forced to begin as integrated refiners as well in order to avoid

---

11. Statement of Donald O'Hara, President of the National Petroleum Refiners Association, *Hearings on the Petroleum Industry,* p. 387. The authors are especially indebted to Mr. O'Hara for his assistance in preparing this section.

12. FTC Staff, *Complaint Counsel's Prediscovery Statement,* p. 13. Peter Bradford, in describing the political machinations accompanying Occidental Petroleum's 1969 application for a special exemption from the oil import quota, reports that the majors entered into an agreement to restrict refinery construction on the East Coast. Such an agreement, of course, would be a clear violation of the Sherman Act. However, Bradford offers no documentation for this charge. See Bradford, Peter A. *Fragile Structures: A Story of Oil Refineries, National Security, and the Coast of Maine.* New York: Harper's Magazine Press, 1975, p. 45.

13. Allvine and Patterson, p. 216.

14. FTC Staff, *Preliminary Report,* pp. 25-27 and *Complaint Counsel's Prediscovery Statement,* pp. 13-21.

15. This argument has a long history in the antitrust literature. See, for example, Kahn, Alfred. "Standards for Antitrust Policy." *Harvard Law Review,* Volume 67, 1953, p. 44; Bain, Joe S. *Barriers to New Competition.* Cambridge: Harvard University Press, 1956, pp. 156-165; Blake, Harlan and Jones, William. "In Defense of Antitrust." *Columbia Law Review,* Volume 65, March 1965, pp. 392-393.

being placed at a competitive disadvantage.[16] This, in turn, raises the already high capital requirements for entry.

Just how effective have the majors been in keeping new entrants out of refining? Since World War II, ten new refineries have been built that specialize in products like asphalt or lubricating oils.[17] However, most commentators define entry into refining as achieving a capacity of 50,000 bpd or more. In Table 13 we have listed those independents that have entered the refining industry since 1950, using this definition of entry. There are 13 of these companies, of which seven initially acquired existing refineries, while six built new refineries.

Scherer and his associates suggest in a recent study that using 50,000 bpd of capacity as a definition of entry may well understate the extent of new entry in refining. Their research indicates that one way a new company gains entry is through the purchase of a small, perhaps technically obsolete refinery.[18] The new entrant can then make bottleneck-breaking investments that increase output in large increments.[19] We might add that, because of various biases built into government regulations, there are substantial incentives for new entrants to remain small. These biases include the small business set aside for defense procurement, the exemption from purchasing entitlements under the Energy Policy and Conservation Act and, until recently, the sliding scale allocation of import quotas. Whether this has affected the independents' overall share of refining is anyone's guess.

Whatever the definition of new entrants, the Allvine and Patterson charge that no new independent refineries have been built since 1950 is false.[20] The FTC staff, however, has been more careful with its facts. The staff has simply asserted that "there has been no significant new entry into the refining of petroleum products" since 1950.[21] The issue here is: Does the entry of 13 large independents in

---

16. FTC Staff, *Preliminary Report*, p. 26.

17. Information supplied by Donald O'Hara of the National Petroleum Refiners' Association.

18. Scherer, F.M., Beckenstein, A., Kaufer, E. and Murphy, R. *The Economics of Multi-Plant Operation: An International Comparisons Study.* Cambridge: Harvard University Press, 1975, pp. 148-9.

19. One of the best examples of this is Coastal States which bought a 29,000 bpd refinery in the sixties and later expanded it to over 160,000 bpd. Cited in letter to Hon. Phillip Hart from Donald O'Hara, *Hearings on the Industrial Reorganization Act,* p. 6276.

20. Unfortunately, some policy makers have believed this erroneous charge. For example, Senator Gary Hart cited it in Senate debate on divestiture. See 121 *Cong. Rec.* S17690 (daily ed., October 7, 1975).

21. FTC Staff, *Complaint Counsel's Prediscovery Statement,* p. 13.

TABLE 13

COMPANIES ENTERING THE REFINING SECTOR
AND CONSTRUCTING MORE THAN 50,000 bpd OF
NEW CAPACITY SINCE 1950

Company	1975 Capacity (bpd)
*Amerada-Hess	538,500
American Petrofina	200,000
*ECOL (under construction)	200,000
Coastal States	162,982
*Union Pacific	140,453
Murphy	129,500
*Commonwealth	110,000
*Koch	106,990
Tenneco	97,500
Charter	82,900
Toscopetro	71,570
Tesoro	64,000
*Hawaiian Independent	60,000

*Initial entry achieved through construction of a new refinery.

Source: Donald O'Hara, President, National Petroleum Refiners' Association.

the last 25 years qualify as "significant?" We believe it does.

However, the real issue is not whether the number 13 is significant or not. Instead, it is whether the major oil companies have actually erected and maintained entry barriers in refining, and, in particular, whether their vertically integrated structure poses a barrier to entry for independent refiners. This requires a closer examination of the FTC charges.

We begin with charges relating to crude oil supply. Because import quotas and pipeline ownership have already been discussed, we focus on market demand prorationing. The Commission staff argues that market demand prorationing — the system whereby producing states set production levels to "balance" supply and demand — was used by the major oil companies to keep independents out of refining. Prorationing supposedly denied independents an assured supply of crude oil. But the staff never explains exactly how the majors accomplished this feat. This omission is perhaps understandable, for, as McCullough points out, prorationing actually aided the would-be entrant in obtaining crude supplies. Under market demand prorationing, all that was necessary was to petition the state conservation authorities to have the allowable production limitation raised.[22]

The charge that interlocking directorates have been used to deny financing to independent refiners does not pass muster either. For example, Tesoro has grown and prospered over the last ten years partly as a result of loans from the Continental Illinois Bank of Chicago.[23] Yet, Texaco, Continental, and Standard of Indiana all have had directors serving on Chicago Continental's board.[24] A more recent example is the financing of the only new grassroots refinery now under construction in the United States, a 200,000 bpd facility being built by ECOL in Louisiana. Of its total cost of about $365 million, $275 million is being provided by a consortium of 15 banks.[25] This evidence, together with data presented in Table 13, suggests that if interlocking directors have been trying to deny financing to independents through the banking system, they have not been overly successful.

The staff of the Federal Trade Commission also contends that the major oil companies have kept independents out of refining by controlling gasoline marketing. This has been done, it is claimed, by segmenting the market for retail gasoline into two markets, one for branded gasoline and one for nonbranded gasoline, and then restricting the opportunity to supply branded outlets to the majors' refineries and "cooperating independent refineries."

This argument makes little sense. First, we have demonstrated in Chapter 2 that the majors do not control gasoline marketing. Even more difficult to accept is the charge that the major oil companies have divided the gasoline market into branded and nonbranded markets. Excess capacity in refining has led to spot market sales and this, in turn, has done much to create the branded/nonbranded distinction. However, the Federal Trade Commission has also done its part. In 1967, the FTC issued a policy statement that it would not look favorably on companies that priced branded gasoline competi-

---

22. U.S.Senate, Committee on Interior and Insular Affairs, *Department of the Treasury Staff Analysis of the Preliminary FTC Staff Report,* (by Douglas McCullough), Washington, D.C., Committee Print , 1973, p. 51.

23. See "Under the Gun." *Forbes,* September 1, 1975.

24. McDonald, *Interlocking Oil,* pp. 15, 23 and 31.

25. Information supplied by ECOL officials. ECOL is being built by Northeast Petroleum, a large independent marketer in New England, and the Ingram Corporation of Tennessee. Middle South Utilities is purchasing most of ECOL's heavy oils and has provided ECOL with $70 million in advance payments.

tively with nonbranded gasoline.[26] Thus, the FTC has actually helped perpetuate the branded/nonbranded distinction for which it is now prosecuting the major oil companies.

Finally, we consider the charge that vertical integration, by raising capital requirements for new entrants, acts as a barrier to entry. On its face, the proposition seems plausible. It is generally more difficult to convince investors to lend a larger than a smaller sum to a potential borrower.

Yet, this argument, when subjected to closer scrutiny, fails to stand up. If above normal profits are being made in refining, new firms will seek entry. Because of above average profits, potential entrants will be able to offer investors an above average return on their money. No theory of capital market imperfections has been advanced, "which would lead suppliers of capital to avoid areas of higher return to seek areas of lower return."[27]

But, it is argued, established firms have an advantage over the new entrant because they can borrow money at lower interest rates. This lower rate does not reflect any real resource saving because the risk to society, as opposed to the investor, is the same regardless of whether the refinery is built by a potential entrant or an established firm. Instead, the lower rate merely represents a "private and strategic" advantage and is thus a barrier to entry.[28]

There are two problems with this analysis. First, established firms may well be better risks to lenders because of their previous experience. If so, "this element of superiority for the large-scale,

---

26. Cited in Donald O'Hara, "Let's Look at the Record," speech before Symposium on the Energy Crisis sponsored by the Oil, Chemical and Atomic Workers Union, Washington, D.C., March 14, 1974, p. 12. The FTC's Report has been criticized for being more concerned with competitors than with competition. See, for example, Dixon, D.F. "The FTC Report on Gasoline Marketing: A Comment," *The Antitrust Bulletin,* Volume 13, pp. 105-127; see also Gregory, Frank "A Survey of the Price Discrimination Aspects of the Federal Trade Commission's Report on Gasoline Marketing." *Ibid.,* pp. 767-801.

27. Bork, "Vertical Integration and Competitive Process," p. 148.

28. Kahn, Alfred E. *The Economics of Regulation, Volume II.* New York: John Wiley and Sons, 1971, p. 261, note 22. Scherer believes the difference results from investors seeking to save "some subjective anguish by knowing their capital is in steady, time-tested hands." Scherer, pp. 100-01. Of course, if this is the case, the savings in mental anguish are a real resource savings. See McGee, John S. "Efficiency and Economic Size." Goldschmid, Mann, and Weston, eds. *Industrial Concentration: The New Learning.* Boston: Little, Brown & Co., 1974, p. 78.

older firm is properly recognized by the capital markets."[29] Second, the risk to society is identical in both cases *only* if society (and lenders) have identical information on the abilities of both established firms and new entrants. Collecting information on the abilities of would-be entrants is expensive, more expensive than collecting information on existing firms. This difference in information costs results in the difference in interest rates.[30]

In summary, there have been and continue to be barriers to entry in refining. However, these barriers do not appear to have been insurmountable. Nor have they been the result of the sinister workings of the major oil companies. Instead, they are a result of technological and economic factors inherent in the refining business. Or, they are a product of often misguided or uninformed government regulation. In short, these barriers will not be lowered by breaking up or otherwise prosecuting the major oil companies.

29. Harold Demsetz, "Two Systems of Belief about Monopoly." Goldschmid, Mann, and Weston, *Ibid.*, p. 173. Kahn admits that part of the difference in interest rates may be explained by this factor, but contends that part can only be explained by private and strategic advantage. However, he suggests no way empirically of separating the effects of these two causal factors.

30. Cf., Stigler, George J. "Imperfections in the Capital Market." *Journal of Political Economy*, Volume 75, June 1967, p. 291.

CHAPTER TWELVE

Oil Industry Profits

The evidence presented thus far does not support the widely held view that the oil industry is monopolistic. What about the industry's profits? Generally, when monopoly exists, profits are abnormally high. But, as Mitchell notes, ". . . the connection between monopoly and profits is a highly qualified one. Perhaps the strongest statement that can be made is that the persistence of abnormally high profits over long periods of time in a particular industry makes it more likely that the industry is monopolistic than competitive."[1]

Extraordinarily high profits over the long run may indicate circumstances other than monopoly. For example, an industry may be subject to abnormal risk. As a result, companies in that industry require a higher long-run average rate of return than do companies involved in less risky undertakings. Or, for some reason, an industry may have extraordinarily competent managements. The higher profits of the industry may simply reflect the greater effectiveness of its managers. In other words, a high rate of profits over the long run is only an indication and not proof of monopoly.

It has become fashionable to condemn oil companies for their exorbitant profits. While one Senator calls the oil industry's profits "unconscionable" and "indecent," another claims that the oil companies are "selling less but making more." To the man on the

---

1. Mitchell, Edward J. *U.S. Energy Policy: A Primer.* American Enterprise Institute: Washington, D.C. 1974, p.90.

street, recent profit reports by the oil companies are proof that the public has been ripped off.

Needless to say, such simplistic thinking is likely to fall short of the truth. First, historically the oil industry has not been especially profitable. The rate of return of the oil industry has been, over the long run, just about equal to the average rate of return for all U.S. industry. Second, recent "windfall" profits were neither so high as critics have claimed, nor have they been sustained. Third, oil company profits must be higher than they have been in the past. The oil industry is a rising cost industry and will be able to finance higher rates of investment only if its profits improve.

One test of the oil industry's profitability is to compare its return to investors with the return to investors in other industries. Two measures are useful for this purpose. One is the rate of return on investment (ROI). The ROI measures dollar profits as a percentage of the combined debt and equity investment. Table 14 presents ROIs for 29 manufacturing industries over four different time periods. During all four periods oil industry profitability was only slightly above the average for all manufacturing industries. If, on this finding, regulation of the oil industry can be justified, then so can regulation of the drug, tobacco, automobile, and printing and publishing industries.

A second measure of profitability is the after-tax return on stockholders' equity (ROE).[2] The results of a study by *Forbes Magazine*, presented in Table 15, suggest that the energy industry's return on equity, as well as its return on investment, was very near the average for all industry. Interestingly, in their five-year average return on equity, natural gas utilities have, according to the *Forbes* survey, done somewhat better than energy companies as a group. Perhaps there are advantages in being regulated as utilities.

Prior to 1974, oil industry profits were not excessive. However, this does not answer charges that the oil companies have profiteered from shortages created by the Arab embargo and price increases by OPEC. During and after the embargo, oil companies realized

---

2. The financial statements of many companies in the petroleum industry are not readily comparable with statements of companies in other industries because of the method of accounting used by most major oil companies. "Because of the understatement of the asset and equity accounts caused by this method of accounting, one of the most common business profits 'yardsticks'—'return on equity'—cannot be computed for petroleum companies on a comparable basis with other industries." Testimony of Randal B. McDonald, Partner, Arthur Anderson & Co., *Hearings on Market Performance,* pt. 5, p. 18. Mr. McDonald goes on to say that, between 1968 and 1972, the ROE of petroleum companies, when based on full cost accounting, averaged about 25 percent less than the ROE for all manufacturing companies.

substantially greater returns from their operations. According to the First National City Bank of New York, oil industry profits for the first half of 1974 were 60 percent higher than for the first half of 1973.[3] This increase was more than twice as large as the 26 percent average increase recorded for all industries. For this reason, many critics have concluded that the recent surges in profits are the result of gouging by the majors made possible by shortages of oil.

There is no question that these increases were substantial. However, were they unconscionable? To some extent, higher profits during 1973-74 were a statistical illusion. For most oil companies, higher profits in the second half of 1973 and 1974 followed extraordinarily low profits in 1972 and the first half of 1973. Had profits been expressed as a percentage change from the median, or a five- or ten-year average, the rate of increase would have been much lower.

Another way to assess the industry's "windfall" gains is to compare them with performance in other industries. In 1973, the oil industry as a whole registered a 53 percent increase in profits over 1972[4] By contrast, during the same period, the metal working machinery industry realized a 396 percent increase. In the primary non-ferrous metals industry and in the aircraft and parts industry, the profit increases were 101 and 109 percent respectively. The oil industry ranked tenth out of 29 industries examined in a recent Treasury Department study of the change in profits between 1972 and 1973. The rate of increase in its profits was above average; however, it was not extraordinary.

Before passing judgment, one should also break down the increase in profits into its components. Most of the recent increase has either resulted from business other than the production, refining and sale of oil or was due to circumstances beyond the control of the oil companies.

First, most of the increase in the profits of the large integrated oil companies resulted from a substantial increase in the value of inventories held by the companies. This, in turn, was caused by inflation, devaluation of the dollar and the OPEC price hikes. However, when these inventories are replaced at now higher prices, the inventory profits will disappear. Likewise, when the dollar was devalued in 1973, those oil companies with foreign assets realized a further accounting profit. All real property and cash denominated in a foreign currency was immediately worth more in dollars. What is

---

3. Cited in testimony of the Honorable William E. Simon, Secretary of the Treasury, *Hearings on Oil Profits*, p. 130.

4. The following discussion draws heavily on an unpublished study of industry profits prepared by the Treasury Department in mid-1974.

TABLE 14
RETURN ON INVESTED CAPITAL
MANUFACTURING INDUSTRIES

Industry	16-Year Average 1958-73		10-Year Average 1964-73		5-Year Average 1969-73		3-Year Average 1971-73	
	Percent	Rank	Percent	Rank	Percent	Rank	Percent	Rank
Average, all Manufacturing Industries	9.3		9.8		9.4		9.6	
Drugs	16.7	1	17.0	1	17.0	1	16.9	1
Instruments and related products	13.6	2	14.5	2	13.6	2	13.7	2
Motor vehicles and equipment	13.0	3	12.9	3	11.4	4	12.9	3
Tobacco manufacturers	11.8	4	12.0	4	12.0	3	12.3	5
Transportation equipment	11.4	5	11.3	5	9.8	10	10.9	7
Chemicals and allied products	11.0	6	11.1	6	11.1	5	11.6	6
Printing and publishing	10.0	7	10.5	7	10.5	7	10.4	9
Petroleum Industry	**10.0**	**8**	**10.3**	**9**	**10.2**	**8**	**10.4**	**8**
Electrical machinery, equipment and supplies	9.7	9	10.0	11	9.5	12	9.6	14
Other machinery	9.6	10	10.4	8	9.7	11	9.8	13
All manufacturing corporations	9.4	11	9.8	12	9.5	13	9.9	11
Basic chemicals	9.3	12	9.3	16	9.0	16	9.6	15

(Continued)

Industry								
Lumber and wood products except furniture	8.9	13	10.0	10	10.9	6	12.8	4
Food and kindred products	8.8	14	9.3	15	10.0	9	10.0	10
Furniture and fixtures	8.6	15	9.7	13	9.3	15	9.8	12
Rubber and miscellaneous plastic products	8.5	16	8.9	19	8.5	19	9.1	18
Metalworking machinery and equipment	8.4	17	9.5	14	7.5	23	6.4	29
Other fabricated metal products	8.4	18	9.3	17	8.6	18	9.0	19
Stone, clay, and glass products	8.3	19	8.3	24	8.3	20	9.3	17
Apparel and other finished products	8.2	20	8.9	18	8.7	17	8.8	20
Miscellaneous manufacturing	8.2	21	8.6	21	8.2	21	8.1	21
Primary nonferrous metals	8.0	22	8.4	23	7.7	22	7.0	25
Alcoholic beverages	7.9	23	8.9	20	9.4	14	9.5	16
Aircraft and parts	7.8	24	8.0	25	6.8	26	7.5	22
Leather and leather products	7.8	25	8.5	22	7.1	25	6.6	27
Paper and allied products	7.6	26	7.8	26	7.5	24	7.4	23
Primary metal industries	7.1	27	7.2	27	6.8	27	6.7	26
Textile mill products	6.6	28	7.2	28	6.6	28	7.1	24
Primary iron and steel	6.4	29	6.4	29	6.1	29	6.5	28

Source: Testimony of the Honorable William A. Simon, Secretary of the Treasury, *Hearings on Oil Profits and their Effects on Small Business and Capital Investment Needs of the Energy Industries before the Subcommittee on Government Regulation of the Senate Select Committee on Small Business*, 93d Congress, 2d Sess. 1974, P. 145, based upon information provided by the Federal Trade Commission.

TABLE 15

PROFITABILITY OF VARIOUS U.S. MANUFACTURING INDUSTRIES

	RETURN ON EQUITY			RETURN ON TOTAL CAPITAL		
	5-Year Average (percentage)	Industry Rank	Latest 12 months (percentage)	5-Year Average (percentage)	Industry Rank	Latest 12 months (percentage)
Consumer Goods: Health Care	17.2	1	17.1	15.1	1	14.5
Consumer Goods: Personal	14.5	2	15.8	13.3	2	10.8
Financial	14.3	3	14.0	7.3	23	6.8
Leisure & Education	13.9	4	14.3	10.2	5	10.5
Construction & Drilling	13.1	5	12.9	8.2	15	9.2
Consumer Goods: Food & Drink	12.9	6	13.1	9.5	9	9.8
Distribution: Retailers	12.8	7	12.3	9.7	8	9.9
Banks	12.6	8	12.9	10.9	4	9.9
Utilities: Natural Gas	12.6	8	11.9	6.9	26	6.9
Consumer Goods: Household	12.2	10	12.9	9.2	10	9.7
Distribution Wholesalers	12.1	11	13.3	10.0	6	9.9
Nonferrous Metals	11.8	12	12.0	8.7	13	9.3
Electronics	11.7	13	13.8	10.0	6	11.3
Insurance	11.7	13	11.5	11.6	3	11.7
Information Processing	11.4	15	11.5	8.8	11	8.9

(Continued)

Multicompanies Conglomerates	11.2	16	13.1	7.7	21	7.8
Utilities: Electric & Telephone	11.1	17	10.9	5.8	27	5.8
Automotive	11.0	18	12.7	8.6	14	9.0
Energy	**11.0**	**18**	**13.0**	**8.2**	**15**	**9.3**
Industrial Equipment	11.0	18	12.1	7.8	19	8.3
Aerospace & Defense	10.9	21	10.9	7.7	21	7.1
Building Materials	10.7	22	13.3	8.8	11	10.3
Chemicals	10.5	23	12.8	7.8	19	8.4
Distribution: Supermarkets	10.4	24	8.1	7.9	17	5.8
Consumer Goods: Apparel	9.6	25	10.5	7.2	24	8.2
Multicompanies; Multi-Industry	9.5	26	11.5	7.9	17	9.2
Forest Products & Packaging	9.4	27	12.9	7.1	25	8.1
Steel	6.1	28	9.0	5.1	28	6.5
Transportation: Surface	5.4	29	7.4	4.7	29	4.9
Transportation: Airlines	4.8	30	9.6	3.1	30	5.2
Industry Median	**11.4**		**12.8**	**8.2**		**9.0**
Industry Average	**11.3**		**12.2**	**8.5**		**8.7**

Source: *Forbes*, January 1, 1974, p.112.

significant about these accounting gains is that they were due to nonrecurring events. Barring further increases in the price of crude oil or another dollar devaluation, these gains were a one-time phenomenon. Consequently they are unlikely to generate the cash flow necessary for new capital investments by the industry. Nor are they likely to encourage the long-term investment needed in the industry.

Second, many oil companies are horizontally integrated. As a rule, these companies earned higher profits from businesses other than oil. In 1973, tanker rates soared to record levels. This substantially increased the 1973 profit levels of those oil companies that are also in the tanker business. Also, a strong upturn in demand for petrochemicals in 1973 and early 1974 contributed to the higher profits of those oil companies that are also in the petrochemicals industry.

The Treasury Department has collected information on the profit increases of 19 large oil companies. Its data are presented in Table 16. Between the first quarter 1973 and the first quarter 1974, the total consolidated profits of the 19 representative companies rose 76 percent. Over half of this increase was due to revaluation of inventories. The profits of chemical operations also increased sharply, accounting for another 17 percent of the total increase. Higher profits from tanker operations and gains from currency fluctuations together contributed collectively another eight percent of the increase.

When the profits from nonrecurring events and nonpetroleum activities are aggregated, they account for nearly three-fourths of the total increase in oil industry profits between 1973 and 1974. In other words, once these special circumstances are isolated, the recent increase in profits of the oil industry does not seem so high or pernicious.

Moreover, because these high levels of profits were a result of special circumstances, they have not been sustained. Data presented in Tables 17 and 18 clearly illustrate that since mid-1974 profits of the largest oil companies have not only leveled off, but have declined significantly.[5]

During the third quarter of 1974, profit levels were still supported by higher domestic oil and gas prices and the favorable performance of the petrochemicals industry. However, higher taxes, higher costs,

---

5. It is especially important to realize here that the data in Table 17 obscure the extent of the decline. A company that earned $50 million in 1973 and $100 million in 1974 realized a 100 percent increase. If that same company earned $50 million again in 1975, its profits would fall by only 50 percent. The *Oil and Gas Journal* explained the situation cogently: "Under this system, profit declines can never match 'the obscenity of profit increases." Editorial, *Oil and Gas Journal* August 11, 1975.

TABLE 16

PETROLEUM INDUSTRY PROFITS
19 COMPANY DATA

	First Quarter ($ millions)		Increase ($ mill.) (percent)		Percent of Total Increase
	1973	1974			
Total consolidated corporate profits	1,768	3,110	1,341	76	100
Inventory profits	14	712	698	4,901	52
Gains from currency fluctuations	16	65	49	315	4
Profits (losses) on tanker operations	(9)	50	59	n/c	4
Profits on chemical operations	94	315	221	236	17
Other nonpetroleum profits (losses)	7	(27)	(34)	n/c	(3)
Petroleum profits, ongoing operations	1,646	1,994	348	21	26

Source: Testimony of the Honorable William A. Simon, Secretary of the Treasury, *Hearings on Oil Profits*, p. 136, based upon information provided by the Department of the Treasury. n/c means that the rate of increase cannot be calculated meaningfully.

lower demand for products, lower production rates, and the absence of further substantial inventory profits began taking their toll. The rate of increase in profits began slowing down noticeably.[6]

By the fourth quarter 1974, oil profits were actually falling. A strong chemical sector and higher prices for crude oil and natural gas tended to bolster earnings. However, declining international earnings and softer domestic demand, together with lower refined product prices, higher taxes and rising costs largely offset these gains. Indeed, the poor fourth quarter pulled projected 1974 earnings down for nearly all major oil companies. Significantly, the

---

6. *Oil and Gas Journal.* November 11, 1974, p. 124.

TABLE 17

NET PROFITS OF LEADING U.S. OIL COMPANIES
(MILLIONS OF DOLLARS)

Rank By Assets	Company	4th Quarter 1973	1st Quarter 1974	2nd Quarter 1974	3rd Quarter 1974	4th Quarter 1974	1st Quarter 1975	2nd Quarter 1975	3rd Quarter 1975
1	Exxon	784.0	705.0	850.0	800.0	778.0	590.0	535.0	550.0
2	Texaco	453.5	589.4	460.4	378.4	319.8	178.4	175.6	232.8
3	Mobil	271.6	258.6	367.4	277.8	136.3	186.2	195.7	231.0
4	Gulf	230.0	290.0	250.0	275.0	185.0	195.0	160.0	175.0
5	Socal	283.1	293.0	285.0	299.5	293.0	169.0	183.4	191.0
6	Amoco	121.4	219.0	280.0	296.5	174.8	146.2	232.0	213.0
7	Tenneco	80.9	84.0	---	73.4	76.4	73.0	---	---
8	Arco	91.7	93.9	139.7	144.0	96.9	67.5	70.4	98.1
9	Shell	79.4	121.8	124.5	216.0	158.2	104.4	118.0	159.8
10	Continental	89.3	109.1	100.4	120.2	61.8	69.4	77.9	82.6
11	Sun	75.0	90.8	127.3	105.7	54.0	33.3	53.3	73.7
12	Phillips	86.7	80.9	123.8	112.9	84.5	54.7	111.2	72.3
13	Union	51.0	73.0	79.6	79.9	55.5	40.1	42.0	82.2
14	Occidental	---	67.8	92.6	86.8	---	73.8	43.7	29.4
15	Getty	52.6	73.6	62.2	86.5	58.6	41.0	68.3	58.5

(Continued)

16	Cities Service	42.1	68.8	53.8	45.8	46.4	27.0	24.2	39.9
17	Sohio	11.6	22.6	50.3	37.0	28.6	22.2	38.1	32.7
18	Amerada Hess	104.5	49.8	46.0	38.2	67.8	27.6	33.5	28.9
19	Marathon	46.9	30.6	50.2	48.7	40.9	16.2	32.6	33.4
20	Pennzoil	24.1	41.3	37.6	33.7	--	26.9	26.9	27.1
21	Ashland	34.4	19.4	32.0	27.3	38.6	19.5	26.8	38.0
22	Kerr-McGee	--	23.6	37.4	32.2	31.0	28.0	38.5	32.6
23	Murphy	13.9	25.5	17.9	12.2	13.0	8.6	9.3	10.5
24	Skelly	16.8	19.7	26.9	31.1	35.5	17.0	26.5	24.8
25	Superior	--	14.5	--	--	--	--	--	--
26	American Petrofina	16.7	13.1	--	31.9	22.4	4.6	9.6	16.7
27	Louisiana Land	--	28.0	--	--	--	--	--	--
28	Clark	8.1	--	9.3	(3.4)	(7.6)	--	(2.7)	3.0
	Apco	--	3.0	--	--	--	--	3.0	--
	Commonwealth	--	--	--	(14.7)	--	--	--	--
	Fina	--	--	19.2	--	--	--	--	--
	Mapco	--	8.7	--	--	--	--	--	--
	Quaker State	--	5.3	5.8	--	--	--	6.4	--
	Tesoro	12.6	--	18.9	--	--	--	--	--
	Total of Firms in the Sample:	3,082.0	3,523.9	3,748.2	3,672.6	2,849.5	2,219.7	2,339.1	2,537.0

Source: *Oil and Gas Journal:* February 18, 1974; May 13, 1974; August 12, 1974; November 11, 1974; February 17, 1975; August 11, 1975; November 10, 1975.

TABLE 18

NET PROFITS OF LEADING U.S. OIL COMPANIES

(PERCENTAGE CHANGE FROM THE SAME QUARTER DURING THE PREVIOUS YEAR)

Company	4th Quarter 1973	1st Quarter 1974	2nd Quarter 1974	3rd Quarter 1974	4th Quarter 1974	1st Quarter 1975	2nd Quarter 1975	3rd Quarter 1975
Exxon	59.0	38.8	66.7	25.4	- 1.1	11.4	-34.3	-31.2
Texaco	70.1	123.2	72.1	23.1	-29.5	-66.0	-52.2	-37.9
Mobil	68.2	65.9	99.5	20.2	-51.0	-28.0	-46.7	-16.8
Gulf	98.3	75.7	28.2	31.0	-19.6	-32.8	-49.2	-36.3
Socal	94.2	91.5	56.6	32.6	3.5	8.3	-22.5	-32.7
Amoco	52.7	81.0	130.8	101.3	43.9	-33.2	-17.1	-28.1
Tenneco	14.4	52	---	37.8	-5.5	-13.1	---	---
Arco	47.4	86.7	104.3	140.9	5.7	-28.1	-49.6	-31.8
Shell	-1.5	51.9	39.1	158.4	99.3	-14.3	-5.2	-26.0
Continental	91.6	129.9	106.2	121.8	-30.8	65.2	-17.3	-38.1
Sun	59.6	84.8	163.0	84.5	-28.0	-63.3	-58.2	-30.2
Phillips	127.6	86.4	166.8	109.6	-2.5	-49.6	-10.2	-35.9
Union	55.5	90.7	98.0	57.6	8.8	-45.1	-47.2	2.8
Occidental	---	717.6	292.8	297.3	---	26.3	-45.8	-60.0
Getty	115.0	172.7	167.2	171.9	11.4	-44.3	9.9	-32.3

(Continued)

109

Cities Service	49.8	87.0	76.4	75.5	10.0	-59.0	-49.8	- 7.8
Sohio	-39.9	29.1	18.9	105.6	146.6	-1.8	1.6	-12.0
Amerada Hess	471.9	35.8	38.0	-12.9	-35.1	-44.6	-27.1	-24.3
Marathon	92.8	52.5	147.2	49.9	-27.6	-47.0	-35.0	-31.3
Pennzoil	68.4	110.7	95.0	80.3	--	-12.4	-18.6	-3.2
Ashland	52.2	22.2	44.5	14.2	12.2	12.8	-7.3	12.4
Kerr-McGee	--	98.9	96.4	143.7	65.3	102.3	1.1	-2.6
Murphy	181.0	232.7	52.8	-19.7	-6.8	-40.0	-52.0	-46.4
Skelly	31.3	97.0	198.9	280.0	111.3	-13.7	-1.5	-20.2
Superior	--	208.5	--	--	--	--	--	--
American Petrofina	218.2	176.3	--	247.6	34.0	-64.8	-50.0	-47.6
Louisiana Land	--	79.1	--	--	--	--	--	--
Clark	140.8	--	10.2	-137.5	-193.8	--	-148.8	--
Apco	--	240.1	--	--	--	--	12.0	--
Commonwealth	--	--	--	-281.3	--	--	--	--
Fina	--	--	205.5	--	--	--	--	--
Mapco	--	50.4	--	--	--	--	--	--
Quaker State	--	47.9	22.4	--	--	--	8.8	--
Tesoro	183.5	--	324.2	--	--	--	--	--
Total of Firms in the Sample:	69.9	78.4	80.2	49.8	-7.7	-29.3	-34.5	-2.94

Source: *Oil and Gas Journal:* February 18, 1974; May 13, 1974; August 12, 1974; November 11, 1974; February 17, 1975; May 5, 1975; August 11, 1975; November 10, 1975.

five "international giants" performed less satisfactorily than firms that had invested predominantly in the United States.[7]

Reports for 1975 indicate that the profits erosion has continued. At the end of the first quarter, for example, *Petroleum Intelligence Weekly* reported:

> Profits for large United States oil firms with mainly domestic operations followed closely the trend set by the American international majors; sagging demand and slackening chemical operations took their toll. In the aggregate, profits tumbled 33 percent for 12 large, mainly domestic firms. This compares with a 30.4 percent decline for the five U.S. international majors.[8]

The major reason for the spectacularly poor performance in 1975 was the elimination of the percentage depletion allowance for the largest oil companies. Some firms were hurt by the Administration's Old Oil Entitlements Program and increases in the crude oil import license fee. Slack demand for many refined products also contributed to lower profit levels.[9]

During the second and third quarters of 1975 domestic companies did somewhat better than U.S.-based internationals. However, the profits of almost all companies were substantially lower than in comparable quarters of 1974. The reason: the same as before—government policies and slack demand for products.[10]

One final point deserves attention here. Throughout 1973 and into 1974, it appeared that the integrated international oil companies were realizing greater profits on foreign than domestic operations. The principal reason for this was stronger demand and tighter supply abroad than at home. Especially in Europe, the international oil companies suddenly realized profits on foreign refining and marketing operations which had not been realized for years. Fortunately for the United States, this situation has not persisted. By mid-1974, there was considerably less divergence between the foreign and domestic profit rates of the major international oil companies. Whether this will continue depends, to no small extent, on the policies of the U.S. Government.

By most recent estimates, the future capital needs of the

---

7. *Oil and Gas Journal.* February 17, 1975, pp. 38-39.

8. *Petroleum Intelligence Weekly.* May 5, 1975, p. 5.

9. *Ibid.,* Profits increased significantly during the first quarter of 1975 for one of the largest oil companies, Continental. This was a result, primarily, of its heavy investment in coal. The coal industry, now free from government price controls, has been performing reasonably well.

10. *Petroleum Intelligence Weekly.* August 4, 1975, p.4 and November 3, 1975, pp. 8-9. See also *Oil and Gas Journal,* August 11, 1975, p. 26.

petroleum industry will be formidable.[11] Because it is tied to an increasingly scarce resource, the oil industry faces increased production costs over time. In 1973, the Chase Manhattan Bank estimated that, in order to meet its projected capital requirements, the petroleum industry will need an annual increase in after-tax profits of 18 percent for the next fifteen years.[12] Over the past fifteen years, the industry's after-tax profits increased by only 7.6 percent annually. Put differently, the petroleum industry will require a 16.5 percent return on equity for the next fifteen years compared to the average 10.6 percent return on equity realized during the previous fifteen years. If the oil companies are to meet anticipated demand for their products, their operations must become more, not less profitable.

In conclusion, the oil industry has not been especially profitable. It has, in fact, done scarcely better than the average for all industry. Two years ago the industry enjoyed a substantial increase in profits. However, it then suffered a substantial drop in profits, something its detractors, particularly those in the Congress, seem to have ignored. Yet, industry profits must improve substantially if the supply of petroleum products is to keep pace with demand and the nation is to become reasonably self-sufficient in oil.

---

11. See Hass, Mitchell and Stone, Chapter 3.

12. Chase Manhattan Bank, "The Energy Shortage and Worldwide Energy Needs," New York City: Chase Manhattan Bank, 1973.

Conclusion

There would seem to be little reason for special regulations being imposed on the oil industry other than normal antitrust laws generally applicable to all industries. The oil industry is one of the least concentrated in the United States. There is no evidence that the major oil companies have expanded their share of the marketplace at the expense of independents. Indeed, the evidence, if anything, suggests the opposite. Nor, as a rule, does it seem that the majors have used vertical and horizontal integration, joint ventures, exchange and processing agreements, or interlocking directorates to engage in anticompetitive practices. Finally, oil industry profits, when viewed in their historical perspective, have not been excessive; nor were recent short-lived increases in profits "unconscionable."

Why, then, are the major oil companies everyone's villain? What has brought about the current state of affairs where Congress and a number of state legislatures seem determined to enact punitive legislation that can only discourage needed investment by the major oil companies and dissuade them from doing what is necessary if the national goal of greater self-sufficiency in oil is to be achieved?

One important reason can be summarized in a word — size. Big oil *is* big. And it is also highly visible. In terms of total sales, four of the top ten, eight of the top 25, and twelve of the top 50 companies in the United States are major oil companies. (See Table 19.) In terms of assets, net income, stockholders' equity and total profits, the presence of the majors among the largest U.S. companies is even more pronounced. Yet, if one looks at measures that might indicate

113

TABLE 19

1973 OIL COMPANY RANKINGS ACCORDING TO:

Domestic Company	Sales	Assets	Income	Stockholders Equity	Profits	Net Income as Percent of Sales	Net Income as Percent of Stockholders Equity	Growth Rate of Earnings Per Share	Total Return to Investors
Exxon	2	1	1	1	2	45	66	258	74
Texaco	6	3	4	4	5	24	99	257	177
Mobil	7	7	6	7	7	103	141	167	235
Gulf Oil	10	9	8	8	9	44	157	260	130
Standard of California	11	10	7	6	8	31	149	255	137
Standard of Indiana	15	12	13	9	14	46	246	190	56
Shell Oil	18	16	16	16	18	123	325	357	45
Continental Oil	21	26	29	26	32	165	190	238	26
Arco	26	17	24	15	25	124	400	290	19
Occidental Petroleum	36	32	108	62	91	404	393	163	275
Phillips Petroleum	40	27	81	23	34	91	270	334	13
Union Oil	49	31	39	28	48	113	334	178	38

Source: *Fortune*, May 1974, pp. 232-235; *Forbes*, May 15, 1974, pp. 229-250.

the presence of monopoly, such as net income as a percentage of both sales and stockholders' equity, or total return to investors, the major oil companies have generally lagged behind other large companies.(Again, see Table 19.) Exxon, which is second in sales and first in assets among industrial corporations, is 74th in total return to its investors. Mobil, which is seventh in both sales and assets, ranks 235 in return to its investors. Bigness is not a crime — at least at present.[1] The evidence strongly suggests that the major oil companies' bigness has not been associated with anti-competitive behavior.

Another reason is politics. The oil industry is a highly visible target for many politicians, especially many congressmen. Why? Because, as one perceptive observer of the Washington scene has noted:

> [M]any congressmen are continuously surveying their political horizons in search of issues with which they can become personally identified and which can become the basis of sub-committee chairmanships, highly publicized hearings, and state or national visibility.[2]

Leading the drive to break-up the "monopolistic" oil industry presents such an opportunity. Many cannot resist it.

The regulatory and punitive face of federal energy policy continues to dominate federal energy policy and threatens to become more dominant in the future. Even the Federal Energy Administration has been preoccupied with regulation at the expense of other national goals, particularly increased productive capacity and greater self-sufficiency in oil.[3] There is now growing concern over whether the current climate is sufficiently conducive for the major oil companies to undertake needed investment in the industry.[4] The emphasis on punitive measures against the majors not only has no basis in fact, it is likely to be highly detrimental to the nation. While the Congress and the Administration mete out punishment to the major oil companies, OPEC and the Arab producing nations can only chuckle.

---

1. "[T]he law does not make mere size an offense." *United States v. United States Steel Corporation,* 251 U.S. 417, 451 (1920).

2. Wilson, James Q. "The Politics of Regulation." McKie, ed. *Social Responsibility and the Business Predicament.* Washington, D.C: The Brookings Institution, 1974, p. 145.

3. This theme is developed further in Johnson, William A. "Federal Energy Policy: A Conflict of Interest" in Kalter and Vogley, eds.

4. For example, see *Oil and Gas Journal.* December 16, 1974, p. 26 and December 30, 1974, pp. 71-76.